THE ROCK OF OUR SALVATION

THE ROCK OF OUR SALVATION

by

Lachlan Mackenzie of Lochcarron

REFORMATION PRESS

2017

British Library Cataloguing in Publication Data

ISBN 978-1-872556-26-0

© Reformation Press 2017

Originally published in 1849 as *Sermons preached at Lochcarron, Ross-shire, by the late Rev. Lachlan Mackenzie, Minister of that Parish, with Memoir by his Sister and Preface by the Rev. W. Mackenzie, Free Church, North Leith.* This edition edited by Dr Robert J Dickie

Published by Reformation Press
11 Churchill Drive, Stornoway
Isle of Lewis, Scotland HS1 2NP

www.reformationpress.co.uk

Also available as a Kindle e-book
ISBN 978-1-872556-35-2

Printed by www.lulu.com

Contents

Introduction   7

Preface to 1849 edition   9

Memoir of the Rev. Lachlan Mackenzie   11

Sermon 1   Christ the Rock   27

Sermon 2   The mountain of the Lord   49

Sermon 3   The great and precious promises   68

Sermon 4   Tribulations of the people of God   94

Heaven—Lines occasioned by the death of his sister   123

Introduction

L OCHCARRON is a parish on the west coast of Ross-shire, and it is located in a ruggedly beautiful area of the country. However, the parish was in spiritual darkness under unconverted ministers until 1726 when Æneas Sage went there. At first he met with stiff opposition from the unruly parishioners. Some of them attempted to burn down the barn in which he was lodging the night before his ordination as the minister of the congregation, and he frequently encountered personal violence during the years he laboured there. However, it was the purpose of the Lord that Sage should be minister in that parish and many were converted under his ministry. He remained there until his death in 1774.

After the short six-year ministry of Sage's successor, Donald Munro, Lachlan Mackenzie was inducted to Lochcarron in 1782. He was a man of genius and was distinguished as one of the most eminently pious ministers of his day. Every Lord's Day the church was crowded to the doors with eager hearers. Even the unconverted were awed by him. One of his them could say that he was very careless and ignorant of divine things, nevertheless he felt that the minister was 'truly a man of God. There was a simplicity and heavenliness in all that he said and did, that both impressed and overawed me.'

We can gain some idea of the powerful preaching of the minister affectionately and reverentially known as 'Mr Lachlan' from the four sermons printed in this volume. It was issued in 1849, entitled *Sermons preached at Lochcarron, Ross-shire, by the late Rev. Lachlan Mackenzie, Minister of that Parish, with Memoir by his Sister and Preface by the Rev. W. Mackenzie, Free Church, North Leith*.

For a long time this was the only published record of Lachlan Mackenzie's sermons. It is now reprinted in its entirety, together with the original Preface and the Memoir written by Lachlan Mackenzie's only surviving sister. This reprint by Reformation Press has been lightly edited with some alterations to layout, grammar, punctuation and vocabulary to bring it in line with current usage. Explanations of obscure words have been given in brackets.

The four sermons in this volume are both searching and edifying, and it is the prayer of the publisher that they may be blessed to the souls of readers.

THE PUBLISHER
Stornoway
August 2017

Preface to 1849 edition

THE Reverend Lachlan Mackenzie of Lochcarron was no ordinary man. He has stamped his impress on a large portion of his countrymen. The remarkable contrast between the Highlanders of 1746 and 1845 is in no small degree owing to him. If Dr Macdonald of Urquhart led the clans of the Highlands and Islands under the Christian banner of the Disruption [in 1843], Mr Lachlan's previous labours had a great influence in rescuing their minds from ignorance and barbarism, and bringing them under the power of the gospel. Neither Knox nor the Covenanters influenced the Highland mind. Hog of Kiltearn, Fraser of Alness, the Frasers of Kirkhill, the Calders, the Sages, the Macintoshes, the Bains and the Kennedys, Mr Lachlan Mackenzie, and Dr John MacDonald—those were the evangelists and apostles of the Highlands and Islands. They succeeded to the influence over the minds of their countrymen which the ancient chieftains abused and the modern forfeited. To Mr Hog and Mr Lachlan the Highlanders ascribe something beyond ordinary ministers—high acquaintance with the secret of the Lord, such as the Lowlanders claimed for John Knox and Robert Bruce.

Mr Lachlan was a profound divine, an eloquent preacher, a deeply experienced Christian and, in addition, a classical scholar, a popular poet, a man of original genius, and eminently a man of prayer. Highland evangelists have often descended to the tomb without leaving any written remains or memoir. The following pages are an attempt to preserve some recollections of Mr Lachlan.

This Memoir is compiled from the recollections of his only surviving sister and her son, at one time my nearest neighbour in the ministry. The sermons are from Mr Lachlan's manuscript. Certain statements in the Memoir that seem to claim supernatural gifts for its subject, are susceptible of explanation on different principles, but that such gifts should have been ascribed to him by those of his own day and country prove Mr Lachlan to have been an extraordinary man. When visiting Lochcarron in 1829, my guide assured me that it was his own and the common belief that Mr Lachlan was a prophet.

In my early days, the halo that gilded the declining years of Mr Lachlan, gave him a place of reverence among the Christians of my native town [Inverness], though sixty miles from his parish.

W. MACKENZIE
North Leith
1849

Memoir of the Rev. Lachlan Mackenzie

D URING the greater part of last century the spiritual condition of the West Highlands of Ross-shire, though now much improved, was bordering upon complete moral death. With the exception of a few evangelical ministers, worldliness and indifference to religion characterised the generality of the clergy. When unconcerned preachers held forth a brief hour in the pulpit during the Sabbath day, many of the parishioners often diverted [amused] themselves in the churchyard or collected in the public houses. Such was the state of Wester Ross previous to the labours of the author of the following discourses. It was his happy lot to be a principal instrument in promoting the cause of God and greatly improving the spiritual condition of the people.

The Rev. Lachlan Mackenzie was born in 1754, in Kilmuir Wester, a parish of Ross-shire. His father, Mr Donald Mackenzie, a respectable and intelligent man, and of a very exemplary character, at that time occupied a farm on the property of Kilcoy, in that part of the country, and was connected with some of the first families in the district. His mother, Elizabeth Clark, was a native of the parish of Petty, and was of respectable descent. She was considered a remarkably clever and well-educated woman, and endeared herself exceedingly to the people among whom she resided by her benevolence and substantial acts of kindness, as well as her medical skill, which were often exercised in relieving the needy and the sick.

Mr Lachlan (the distinctive name by which he is known in the Highlands) received the elements of his education in the parish school of Petty, which was taught at that time by an excellent classical scholar. Mr Lachlan was only eight years of age when he was first brought under the power of the truth, and from that time forward his life and conversation continued to shine brighter and brighter unto the perfect day. He was known to have been prevailed upon to engage in the duty of prayer at a meeting in the district before he was thirteen years of age, and even then appeared to have so much solemnity and unction that aged men regretted that, from his youthful modesty, they could not prevail upon him to come forward in public so much as they wished.

He was observed to have the appearance of a solemn sense of the all-seeing eye [of God] upon his spirit all along, in school and at college, as well as in after life. He was kept very humble in early life by the mental and spiritual conflicts he endured, being deeply exercised with a sense of the corruption and wickedness of the heart, the suggestions of unbelief, and the wiles of Satan. Thus he was sent early and late in the day and in the night to his knees before a throne of grace. Few or none in his generation, at least in the part of the country in which he lived, were known to be so earnest or so often engaged in the duty of prayer as Mr Lachlan. And as the psalmist would not engage in battle without first consulting the Lord, so was Mr Lachlan in the habit of seeking and receiving direction in regard even to the most minute actions of life.

We are not certain as to his precise age when he first entered the college of Aberdeen, but we are quite sure that he made a creditable appearance during his whole course at that university, and that his knowledge of the Scripture languages especially was more than ordinary. He was so conversant with his Hebrew Bible that he could use it at family worship. Mr Lachlan taught the parish school of Lochcarron before receiving licence [before he was licensed as a minister], and here his piety began to shine forth in life and conversation [conduct]. His character and sentiments were now beginning to be appreciated by the pious people, not only in the immediate neighbourhood, but also in the surrounding parishes; far and near they flocked to his prayer meetings, and highly esteemed his conversation and company.

'What communion hath light with darkness?' asks the apostle. So, when this light began to appear in the great moral waste, the rulers of darkness not only opposed, but attempted to extinguish it. These trials came upon Mr Lachlan from a quarter whence it would not be expected. The Presbytery of these bounds, instead of encouraging by their approbation such a person as Mr Lachlan, opposed him with their utmost might. The fact was, that his prayer meeting fostered a spirit with which they had no sympathy, and which exposed their own coldness and unfaithfulness.

While Mr Lachlan taught the parish school of Lochcarron, the present manse was built. As he was one evening passing that way, he entered the manse when it was nearly finished. And as prayer was his vital breath and the element in which he lived, he took advantage of the privacy of one of the rooms while the workmen were away, to pour his soul before the Lord, when that passage of scripture (Psalm 60:6) 'I will measure the valley of Succoth', took hold of his mind and would not depart. He inquired what was the meaning of this, and in the course of time he was led to suppose that, as Succoth was a hilly country, the Lord might have some work for him to do at least among the hills and valleys of the Highlands, if not in the place in which he was then residing. That Lochcarron should be the scene of his labours was very unlikely at that time, for there were three members of that Presbytery who tried every means for the purpose of frustrating the hope of his being licensed at all. The ground of their opposition could not have been anything faulty in his character or qualifications, but the hatred they bore to his pious life and evangelical doctrines, with a mixture of jealousy at his constantly increasing popularity. He was kept back more than a year from getting licensed, but when the Lord's time came, all these obstacles were soon removed, and that happened in a way not to have been expected. These three ministers who led the opposition were suddenly and within one year called to go the way of all the earth, and give their account. Mr Lachlan was immediately licensed without any further opposition, and after all a testimony was recorded in the minutes of Presbytery to his high acquirements and character. The people of that neighbourhood, who knew and heard of the whole circumstances, got the impression that it is not safe to treat unjustly any of the true people of God.

Mr Thomas Mackenzie, the proprietor of Applecross, was friendly to Mr Lachlan, as well as to the people upon his own property, and soon procured for him the Crown presentation to the parish of Lochcarron. When this report reached Lochcarron the people were greatly delighted, and to their great joy Mr Lachlan was ordained their pastor, and a door of usefulness was opened for him in the vineyard of the Lord among the hills and valleys of Lochcarron. He then commenced to labour in the means of divine appointment, with intense desires for the best interests of his people but, as has been the case with the most successful ministers, he now felt more than ever that nothing less than the power of God can make people willing to accept of salvation through free grace.

He now began to feel how difficult it was for a minister of Christ to put down the barbarous practices which then prevailed in the Highlands, such as Sabbath profanation, excessive drinking and other vices. But wild as was Lochcarron in those days, it was greatly reformed from the state in which Eneas Sage found it. A brief ministry of six years[1] intervened between Mr Sage and Mr Lachlan. By all accounts Mr Sage was a faithful minister of the Lord—a bold, impartial, and uncompromising reprover of sin—an evangelical preacher of the gospel—and, in addition, a man of immense physical strength. Often did he bear testimony for the cause of God and reprove sin in Lochcarron, where his combined strength and piety alone could command respect and dread. It is to be regretted that the obituary Mr Lachlan wrote of this great and useful man has not been published.

Soon after Mr Lachlan came to Lochcarron he drew out and prevailed upon the people to sign the following regulations, which were no doubt a good preliminary step for improving the state of morality at that time—for after signing the rules they did

---

[1] The original book (1849) incorrectly mentions a ministry of three years. Æneas Sage died on 17th July 1774. His successor, Donald Munro, was ordained on 10th May 1775 and died six years later on 6th August 1781. Lachlan Mackenzie was ordained on 4th April 1782. (Scott's *Fasti Ecclesiæ Scoticanæ*, volume VII, pp. 160–161.) [Editor].

not wholly break through them during his lifetime, and they were more orderly than before in going to Church and returning home on the Sabbath, as well as at burials and on sacramental occasions.

Church of Lochcarron, 26th September 1792

Whereas it is the duty of all who name the name of our Lord Jesus Christ to depart from iniquity, and, as we are desired to abstain from all appearance of evil, we, the after subscribers, conscious that it is our duty to have the cause of God and the interests of religion and morality at heart, finding that great irregularities are practised at burials and other meetings, and even on sacramental occasions; and as we know that other people make an excuse and take an example from the conduct of those who are reputed religious and observing, with regret, that the Sabbath is shamefully profaned by idle talk in the churchyard, have come to the following resolutions, which we are determined, in the strength of God, inviolably to adhere to, *viz.*

1. That none of us will taste a single drop of spirits at a burial after the body is interred. But if the corpse is carried a good distance, and if the day be so coarse as to make it necessary to take a little on the road, that we shall do so at a decent distance from the churchyard, and only take a very little, if necessary, to refresh nature; but, if the day be good, that we shall not take any liquor but what we take at the house from whence the corpse shall be taken; and that, when the body is consigned to the earth, we shall immediately come to our respective homes. And however willing a poor widow may be, from a mistaken principle, to spend a good deal of whisky at the burial of her husband, we are determined that we shall not lay such a burden upon our consciences as to spend wantonly at the burial what might afterwards be of service to the widow and orphans. Whereas any of us singly, from slavish fear, might be afraid to break from this absurd and wicked practice, we hereby resolve, unanimously, to join together in breaking through it, so as that the world cannot be able to lay the blame upon an individual, but upon the whole of us taken collectively.

16

2. We hereby resolve, and promise solemnly and faithfully, in the sight of God, that, if we see or hear of any communicant being the worse of liquor at any meeting, especially a burial or sacrament, we will inform against him, so that he may be proceeded against according to the rules of the Church.

3. That every one of us shall go home immediately after sermon, and not stay in the churchyard conversing on idle or worldly topics.

4. That if any habit or practice, contrary to the word of God, shall be observed in the parish, we shall do our utmost to suppress it.

5. That if any of us, through slavish fear, or a desire to gratify an appetite, shall break through any of these resolutions, he shall be reckoned infamous.

6. And lastly. That, to the utmost of our power, we will endeavour to observe the utmost regularity at our sacramental occasions.

Mr Donald Kennedy, Kishorn, father of the late eminent Mr John Kennedy of Redcastle, was the first name of the hundreds that signed the resolutions.

There were other regulations which he urged upon the people to comply with, such as public baptism [as opposed to private baptism in dwellings]—three regular proclamations of banns before marriage—and that every young man and woman in Lochcarron would know the questions of the Shorter Catechism before asking him to marry them. When a party became displeased and would refuse to obey, Mr Lachlan would say, 'I do not prevent you from taking another minister.' So taking another minister, or lifting the token [communion token] off the table instead of getting it out of his hand, was what few or none liked to do, and when it was done it was well known to be their own fault.

Outward reformation alone was not what Mr Lachlan aimed at chiefly in relation to the people, but the conversion of their souls and preparation for eternity. God often favoured him with visible tokens of the success of his ministry, and that given not in Lochcarron alone, but in many other parts of the county of Ross and Inverness. Many have been known to have come from Sutherland and Argyle, on sacramental and other occasions, to visit Lochcarron for the sake of the gospel, and it will not be known until the great day how great the benefit received by multitudes from the doctrines and prayers of Mr Lachlan.

There were many instances of people attending the fishing at Lochcarron, who were wonderfully caught in the net of the gospel. Two instances of this kind took place by means of Mr Lachlan being directed to mention secret sins they committed, and one of them from being a notorious sinner turned out to be afterwards an exemplary Christian.

Lochcarron was the place where the Lord granted more visible marks of the success of his labours in the ministry, even to people who came from other distant parts of the land. He was often observed to mention and to plead the fulfilment of that promise (Psalm 72:16), 'There shall be an handful of corn in the earth upon the top of the mountains; the fruit thereof shall shake like Lebanon.'

The seed of the kingdom, sown by means of Mr Lachlan's preaching, has borne fruit in various respects. His preaching was the means of awakening, building up, and comforting many. It was a mean [way] of disseminating sound evangelical views of the gospel in that dark part of the land. He was a moral lighthouse to the Western Highlands and Islands, and there need be no doubt (as Dr Begg remarked at the Assembly of Inverness)[2] that his doctrines were a means of leavening the minds of the people with those principles which in that part of the Highlands paved the way for the Disruption. The people of the Highlands saw those principles exemplified in the life as well as doctrines of Mr Lachlan. As he was alone [as an Evangelical minister] in the Presbytery, they [his co-presbyters] sometimes laid a duty upon him that he felt difficult to accomplish, such as the settling of an unacceptable presentee, for the policy of those days was to appoint an influential minister for the purpose of keeping the people quiet and peaceable at the settlement. On one occasion that this task was imposed upon him, he felt the responsibility so great that he delayed obedience, waiting to get light upon the proper path. And although he felt exceedingly grieved on the occasion, the Presbytery had so little consideration and sympathy with him, that the clerk issued a letter to him, threatening to take the legal steps for his deposition. Now, although such conduct was tyrannical on the part of the Church, and contrary to the spirit of the law, Mr Lachlan viewed his ordination vows in that light that he could not disobey the Presbytery without first separating from the Established Church. He therefore did obey, and, writing afterwards to his valuable friend, Dr Ranald Bain of Kiltarlity, about that matter, he said, 'I was that day like blind Samson in the temple of the Philistines. It is true, the presentee to that Gaelic parish did translate a chapter in Isaiah to Gaelic.' The fact of Mr Lachlan's doing this, however, occasioned great uneasiness to him in his latter days.

---

[2] General Assembly of the Free Church of Scotland, 1845.

Instances are still remembered of the efforts of his co-presbyters to thwart his labours for the suppression of sin and promotion of true religion. When Mr Lachlan was sorely tried any time in that way, he would lift his heart in prayer to the Lord, and sometimes send a message to a godly minister to pray for him. On occasion of the Presbytery dining with a rich and influential offender whom Mr Lachlan was subjecting to discipline, when they arranged to defeat his efforts, Mr Lachlan sent a special messenger to the Rev. Charles Calder of Ferintosh, requesting that great and pious minister to sympathize with him and to lay his case before the Lord.

It was no wonder that a godly minister was so treated in a Highland Presbytery in those days, when Mr Calder himself had once to appeal from his own Presbytery to the Synod, to prevent a member of that Presbytery, a Roderick [Rory] Mackenzie, from suppressing a parish by annexation, in order to increase his own emoluments. These were not the days of church extension. Mr Lachlan supported Mr Calder's appeal by a poetical effusion that recorded the event on the minds of his countrymen, and after the Synod of Ross had reversed the deed of the Presbytery suppressing the parish, Mr Lachlan commemorated the circumstance by adding the following stanza:

> The Synod, as it is reported,
> Their character for grace supported;
> And if aright we heard the story,
> None took the Devil's part but Rory.

It was good for these godly ministers that the public usually supported them when their grievances were made known. The weight of public opinion was almost the only protection of the feeble Evangelical minority in the church courts.

Mr Lachlan possessed great powers of satire and repartee, which he thought it his duty on suitable occasions to use in his Master's service. He could employ in the most solemn manner, and in Scripture words, the most cutting irony, and in this he thought himself justified by the example of the prophet (1 Kings 18:27).

Mr Lachlan's large-hearted patriotism compelled him to lift his voice against other acts than those strictly ecclesiastical. He witnessed, with deep concern, that process of depopulation in the Highlands, and the impoverishment of those who were not expatriated. Mr Lachlan alone, of all his brethren, publicly protested against the system. He fearlessly raised his voice against the custom of depopulating parishes for the purpose of making room for sheep walks. He held forth that the soil was intended by the Creator for the maintenance of the human race, and that it was against his law to oppress man to make room for brutes of the inferior creation. He preached a series of sermons at one time from Isaiah 5:8–9: 'Woe unto them that join house to house, that lay field to field, till there be no place, that they may be placed alone in the midst of the earth! In mine ears said the Lord of hosts, Of a truth many houses shall be desolate, even great and fair, without inhabitant.' The honest boldness of this man of God was unpleasant to the sheep farmers, and some of his remarks, on that occasion, were as unwelcome to some farmers and proprietors as Micaiah's faithful prophecies were to Ahab. Mr Lachlan, however, continued to deliver the message he was directed to give, whatever obloquy it drew upon himself. He said that the system would be altered, or that the sheep would be destroyed in a way that was not expected in Scotland. He did not take upon him to determine the times or the seasons of the great alteration which he predicted. But when one in private conversation mentioned to him that many thousands of sheep had been lost in a snow storm, and took occasion to say that Mr Lachlan's predictions were thus in the way of being fulfilled, Mr Lachlan replied, that it was not in this way that he anticipated a change; he was not looking to present appearances—it was neither the snow of winter nor such heat as would dry the tongue of the raven that would bring deliverance from the system of oppression, and grinding the face of the poor. 'But', added he, 'if the people of God be earnest and faithful in prayer, the deliverance will come sooner than it arrived to the children of Israel in Babylon.' This was said in the year 1816, when the new leases were making great changes in Lochcarron.

The people of Lochcarron, besides many others, firmly believed that Mr Lachlan had some special gift or mode of prophecy. Many instances might be mentioned: *inter alia*, the following example. The relater still lives, and is an elder in the Free Church, and affirmed it in the most decided manner two years ago. Mr Lachlan solemnly said from the pulpit, in the hearing of this person, *viz.*, 'Lochcarron young men, go to your knees this evening, and be earnest at a throne of grace. Great is your need to be so. A great breach is to be made upon you. There are five young men present here today that shall be in eternity before this day six weeks, and none of them above twenty-eight years of age.' There was one stranger present that day in the church of Lochcarron, who was a native of Easter Ross, and was then a road contractor in Lochcarron, and he thought with himself, if he lived, that he would mark how this prediction would he verified. It turned out, however, that it was fulfilled in a way he did not look for. There were three young men working for himself at the high road that died suddenly; the rest died in other parts of the parish, within five weeks of the time mentioned. They were all present that day in the church—none of them above twenty-eight years of age. This road contractor was at their burials.

There were many in the Highlands that placed great confidence in what Mr Lachlan would be directed in such a manner to say. They believed him to have been a person who obtained nearness of access to the Lord, and to whom the secrets of the Lord were manifested in a wonderful and uncommon decree. As an instance of the confidence many had in what Mr Lachlan would say, it occurred near Inverness that two gentlemen were crossing in the boat at Kessock ferry during the time that the parish of Redcastle was vacant, before Mr John Kennedy came to it. One of them was a clergyman, and said to the other that the law was decided, and that a certain person was to get the presentation. Another passenger in the boat replied. 'That is impossible.' The minister asked, 'How do you know?' The person answered, 'Because Mr Lachlan said that the gospel would come to Redcastle.' The minister asked, 'What did Mr Lachlan know?'

The other person replied, 'If you speak in that way about such a great and faithful servant of the Lord as Mr Lachlan, I will in the meantime drop the subject. But I call upon you to expose him as much as you can if what he said will not be verified.'

So that minister had not in his power to expose Mr Lachlan on that occasion, for the person that minister mentioned did not get the presentation. And some time thereafter, a minister, of whom he said that the Holy Spirit made a minister of him, was presented to it—the Rev. John Kennedy, who was such an eminent preacher of the everlasting gospel, and countenanced by his divine Master for being so useful in his day and generation, and particularly in the parish of Redcastle.

Mr Lachlan lived singularly above the world while he lived in it. He beheld through faith the glory of spiritual and eternal things to be far greater than the objects of time and sense. There was no man in his generation known to us that so much resembled the life of Elijah or John the Baptist. He was never married, and did not engage in the cares of the world, wishing to be at liberty as an ambassador of the Lord, to give himself wholly to his service. In writing the statistical account of Lochcarron, he said about himself:

> The parson has no horse nor farm,
> Nor goat, nor watch, nor wife.
> Without an augmentation, too,
> He leads a happy life.

So he was a living testimony in his day that religion can render a man happy although he may have but a small competency of the things of this life. He said that the proprietor kindly offered to him a large portion of the district for a farm, but that he refused it, well aware that he could be far happier without it.

Mr Lachlan did not give to his people that which cost him nothing; he was always careful and conscientious in his preparation for the pulpit. But during the first part of his ministry, and at the time he enjoyed the greatest enlargement and liberty, and that he was constantly engaged in public duties in his own parish and in many other places throughout the counties of Ross and Inverness, his chief preparation was meditation and secret prayer.

It was believed by others, and felt and acknowledged by himself, that the doctrines he was delivering at that time were falling like the dew upon his own soul; and what made this so credible to others, was, how troubled souls particularly would get their cases and trials so clearly told to them. For example, a woman in Inverness, who was labouring under great temptations, heard on Saturday that Mr Lachlan was to preach the next Sabbath at Kiltarlity, a distance of more than a dozen miles from Inverness. She went that distance to hear him. Soon, in the course of the sermon, Mr Lachlan said, 'There is a poor soul here whose temptations are very peculiar. You did three things,' he said, and he mentioned them. 'At last you desperately put your hand on the sneck [latch] of the door.' She was amazed by hearing what no fellow-creature knew; and the direction he gave was blessed for consolation as great as her former temptations had been, and to which she was previously a stranger.

There is no evidence that during the first part of his ministry Mr Lachlan wrote out any of his sermons. But towards the decline of life, perhaps feeling more straitened, he began to write his sermons and lectures. This is one reason why his writings are not so rich as the sermons he sometimes delivered in preaching, before he began to write them. His writings contain chiefly, perhaps, the leading ideas on which he preached. After he began the practice, he frequently wrote on the Monday or Tuesday, particularly if he felt a degree of liberty on the Sabbath. It was in this way, we suppose, the following sermon on 2 Peter 1:4, may have been written. But although evidently not intended for publication, it is taken word for word from the original manuscript. The other three sermons we believe to be written in the same manner, but that he afterwards wrote a second copy of them. The last of these sermons was preached on the occasion of the death of Mary, his sister, who was a superior and pious person, and it was on the same occasion that Mr Lachlan composed the lines of poetry at the end of this small volume.

Some of those who heard and knew Mr Lachlan, often expressed regret that no part of his writings was published, hoping that it might be useful. Let the reader judge indulgently of this small specimen of them, taken word for word from his original manuscripts, which were not intended for publication. The following sermons are published from manuscripts in the possession of Mrs Ann Mackenzie, his only surviving sister, who lived with him at the time of his death, and with whom Mr Lachlan had left them, and she subscribes her name to the veracity, according to the best of her knowledge, of all the statements in this brief memoir.

Mr Lachlan was laid aside by a stroke of paralysis fourteen months before his death. Within two or three months before his death, he could not rise or walk without support, but his remarks showed that even then he was feeling that man does not live by bread alone, but by every word which proceedeth out of the mouth of God. Upon the occasion of a person asking him one day how he did, his reply was, 'I am taking a faith's look into heaven.' He departed this life at 11 a.m., 20th April 1819, being the sixty-fifth year of his age, and thirty-seventh of his ministry.

ANN MACKENZIE

Sermon 1

Christit the Rock

That Rock was Christ.
1 Corinthians 10:4

THE design of the apostle is to rectify a mistaken notion in the church of Corinth. They valued themselves upon their privileges, their gifts and their graces. The apostle shows us that these privileges were enjoyed by the church of the Jews. And yet he shows that notwithstanding the great things God had done for them and the great privileges they enjoyed, that many of them were destroyed in the wilderness. He likewise informs us that these things are examples to the Christian church, and he cautions every man who thinks that he stands to take heed lest he fall.

We must not boast of our privileges, for the Jewish church enjoyed the same privileges we do; they ate the same spiritual food, and drank the same spiritual drink—they drank the water of the spiritual Rock, and the Rock was Christ. They had the same sacraments for substance which we have.

In speaking further upon this subject in particular, by divine aid,

1. I shall give a brief account of the history to which this alludes.

2. I shall show in what respects the rock was a type of Christ.

3. As the rock did not yield water till it was struck, in like manner we must strike the Rock of our salvation that we may obtain refreshing streams for our souls.

1. A brief account of the history

I shall give a brief account of the history to which this alludes.

When Moses led the children of Israel into the wilderness of Arabia, they were there but a short time when the people complained for want of water, as we learn from the seventeenth chapter of Exodus. Moses is commanded to bring water out of the rock. Again, thirty-eight years afterwards they fall into the same sin of murmuring. The miracle is repeated. Let us then, for a little, fix our attention and thoughts upon this extraordinary event.

Behold, then, this wonderful sight. Moses is commanded to strike the rock. He goes with the rod of God in his hand, and in the presence of upwards of six hundred thousand men, besides women and children, he prepares himself to work the miracle. The multitude have their expectations raised to the highest pitch. Many of them, no doubt, are full of unbelief, and even Moses himself spoke unadvisedly with his lips. We may naturally suppose that he lifted up his hands and his heart to God in the heavens, and though eminent for his faith in the divine power and in the divine promises, it is probable he might give room to the suggestions of unbelief. He might perhaps say within himself, 'I shall now be put to shame before this great multitude, and what will God do then for his great name? Was it ever heard that God brought water out of a rock before? But silence, my tumultuous thoughts! God hath spoken, and it is my duty to obey. It is true the thing is unlikely, but what is impossible to that power that said, "Let there be light, and there was light," and called forth creation out of nothing. But though nothing is impossible to God, is it likely that he will exert his power to work a miracle in favour of a perverse rebellious people who are always provoking him to anger by their obstinacy and unbelief? I proceed, however, in obedience to the divine command.'

He comes to the rock, and with a strong faith, mixed with a strong unbelief, he strikes the rock in a passion. Behold here a wonderful instance of human weakness! Blessed Moses, the meekest man upon earth, the great favourite of God and the great deliverer of Israel, transported with passion, agitated with unbelief, and tempted at last to speak unadvisedly with his lips.

His faith, however, rises triumphant at last. He strikes the rock twice, the waters flow abundantly like a river—the people are relieved, and God is glorified. But though faith conquers at last, the unbelief and disobedience of the children of God cannot pass unpunished. He is made the glorious instrument of procuring relief to all the people of Israel, and procuring them water for their thirst, but because he gave room to passion and unbelief, he cannot see the Land of Promise, but only gets a transient view of it from the top of Pisgah.

The miracle, however, is a glorious sight—a stroke or two of Moses' rod brings water out of the rock of flint. And it is likely that Moses, at this time, might experience the fate of all popular leaders, for popularity is a bitter sweet. At one time the people speak of stoning him; at another time they extol him to the skies and join in singing the song of Moses and Miriam. Their murmuring is converted into thanksgiving—they believe in God and honour his servant Moses. We may well suppose they sung hallelujahs to the God of Israel for this great salvation. They were like to die for thirst, and now they are relieved by seasonable and refreshing streams. The water ran like a river. There was enough, and more than enough, for the whole congregation. They might now say with truth and propriety, 'What people is like unto thee, O Israel? Thou hast thy manna from heaven, and copious and salutary streams from the rock of flint.' And may we not likewise suppose that the true Israel among the people would be encouraged from this astonishing event to plead that God would bring water out of the rock in their hearts and melt them into true repentance and godly sorrow for sin?

2. The rock was a type of Christ

I proceed to show, in the next place, in what respects the rock was a type of Christ.

The apostle here tells us that 'the Rock was Christ', in the same way in which it is said of the sacramental bread, that it is the body of our Lord. The rock signified or was a type of Christ.

1. The rock did not naturally contain water. Christ had no form or comeliness to the carnal eye. He was a poor man, and a weak man, and crucified in weakness. His cross was a stumbling block to the Jews, and to the Greeks foolishness. The gospel is hid to those who are lost, but the power of God for salvation to those

who believe. Christ is the headstone of the corner to the Church, but the Rock of salvation is a rock of offence to unbelievers and disobedient persons. To the Jews the cross was a stumbling block—they looked for a carnal Messiah, a great conqueror who was to subdue the world under them. They looked upon such promises or scriptures as these—'Gird thy sword upon thy thigh, O thou most mighty, with thy glory and thy majesty' and 'he shall rule from sea to sea, and from the river to the ends of the earth'—merely in a temporal view. They had heard of the conquests of Nebuchadnezzar, or of Cyrus the deliverer of their church, the victories of Alexander the Great, and the Caesars of Rome. They supposed that their Messiah would be greater then all these great conquerors. They hoped he would set up his standard in Jerusalem, the royal city of his ancestors—that he would lead his kinsmen the Jews to conquest and to triumph, that all nations would yield to his victorious arms, and that his enemies would lick the dust. They expected riches, honours and pleasures under the reign of Messiah. How were they disappointed, therefore, when Jesus of Nazareth spoke to them of another kingdom and of other victories! They could not reconcile the mean circumstances in which he appeared to the exalted views they formed of the Messiah whom they expected.

This, then, was a stumbling block to them, not considering that the Messiah must suffer before he was to reign. That there are temporal promises made to the Jewish nation as such, none that reads the Old Testament can deny. And if the Jews had yielded obedience to the Saviour as the promised Messiah, the promises would have begun to operate. It was promised to Abraham that he would have a son, and that his posterity would possess the land of Canaan. This promise was not accomplished till four hundred years thereafter. As their possessing the land of Canaan was suspended [made to depend] upon the condition of obedience to the revealed will of heaven, so if the Jewish nation had embraced the Lord Jesus Christ upon the terms of the gospel they might have continued yet in their own land. They did not look upon him as the proper person to fulfil God's promises to them, and they fulfilled the word of God by rejecting him. His being the Messiah appeared as unlikely to them as it did to their unbelieving ancestors that the rock would supply them with water. The Rock of salvation is to them still a rock of offence, and till they believe that Jesus of Nazareth is the promised Messiah, they must die for want of spiritual water. And when they shall be persuaded to strike the Rock of their salvation, they shall obtain refreshing streams to their souls.

But again, to the Greeks the cross of Christ was foolishness. The apostles were sent to preach the gospel to the Gentiles— the doctrine appeared foolishness to them. The doctrine they preached was that 'God so loved the world that he gave his only begotten Son, that whosoever believeth in him might not perish, but have eternal life.' That the Lord Jesus Christ was the Son of God—that he was born of a virgin, in a stable, in the town of Bethlehem—that he was laid in a manger—that he lived a poor man—that he wrought at the carpenter business, with Joseph his reputed father, till he was thirty years of age—that he began then to preach the gospel—that he was crucified between two thieves—that he was buried, and rose from the dead—that this is the Saviour whom God sent into the world, that such as believe in him will be saved: such as do not believe will be damned. This doctrine, though supported by miracles, appeared foolishness to them. It was as unlikely a method of salvation as it was for the unbelieving Israelite to get water out of a rock to quench his thirst. The Israelite, however, must die for thirst if he did not get water out of the rock, and the sinner must die if he does not accept of salvation through Christ.

2. As the rock yielded water, Christ is a well of water, springing up unto everlasting life, to all that believe. Grace is often compared to refreshing streams of water. From the Rock of salvation proceeded the well of salvation. Nothing can be more grateful and refreshing to the weary traveller than water— nothing so comfortable to the soul as grace. The water refreshed and strengthened the children of Israel in the barren desert. In like manner, the salutary [health-giving] streams that flow from the river of life make glad the city of God. With joy, therefore, we may now draw water out of the wells of salvation. The promises of the gospel are full of consolation to sinners, and the waters of the sanctuary are for health or medicine.

3. The rock did not yield water till it was struck, and that by Moses. No other staff could bring water out of the rock but the rod of Moses. In like manner, Christ was struck by the law of God. He was made a curse. Our sins were upon him. Sin brings the curse of God upon the sinner. All our sins were laid upon the Rock of our salvation, and this brought down all the curses of the broken law upon the Son of God. The law struck him: as we broke all the commandments of the law, they poured all their curses upon his head. All our breaches of the divine law were imputed to him, and every command gave its own stroke. Every several [single] stroke fetched water out of the Rock. The justice of God found our sins upon him, and this drew all the curses of the law upon him. Every sin procured him a curse, and every curse procured him a stroke. But every curse with which the law struck him procured blessings upon blessings for his church and

people. The law cursed him, and he blessed them. He was wounded for our sins, and bruised for our iniquities, the chastisement of our peace was upon him, and with his stripes we are healed. The rock in the wilderness got but a stroke or two; he got many.

Though the children of Israel were like to die for thirst, they cannot get water till Moses strikes the rock. The people might wander ever so long through the wilderness, but they cannot get relief but by striking the rock for them. Mankind may use other means, but there is no salvation in any other name, nor any way of procuring grace for their souls, but through the merits of Christ. He is the way, the truth, and the life, and no man can come unto the Father but in and through him; for without him we can do nothing. It is true, indeed, the nobles digged with their staves, and the people sung, 'Spring up, O well; sing ye to it.' But though this was a duty, it was Moses' striking the rock that procured water. It is our duty to use our poor endeavours, but it is not endeavours or duties that give us the favour of God, but the merits of Christ alone. He is the first and the last, the Alpha and Omega, in the great work of our salvation.

4. The rock gave water not for one or two only, but for all the congregation. This water was not for the benefit of a few favourites among the people of Israel, such as Moses and Aaron, Caleb and Joshua—all the congregation had a right to drink of the water. In like manner, the benefits of the Redeemer's death extend to all the ends of the earth. The gospel feast is a feast for all nations. No Israelite was excluded from that water—no sinner is excluded from this feast, if he does not exclude himself. Any man whatever that comes to take it, is welcome to the water of life. The water of life is free and open

for all. The streams that flowed from the rock ran in such abundance that there was enough and to spare for all the people.

The gospel is free to all. It is not the monopoly of one kingdom, of one country, or people. It is for the general benefit of mankind, and the day is approaching when it shall be sent to all the ends of the earth. When the water gushed out of the rock at first, such of the people as were nearest got the first drink, but in a short time the whole of them had access to the precious blessing. In the first ages the water of life was like a small rivulet, and few had access to drink—it is now like a large refreshing stream, making glad the city of God, and planted with trees on each side of it, and the leaves of the trees, as well as the waters of the river, for the healing of the nations.

Every man in the congregation was welcome to come and drink. We do not read that any man was excluded. Let us make the supposition that some melancholy Israelite made use of the same preposterous reasoning that several poor sinners use against themselves under the gospel. Let us put the case that he appeared before Moses, and told him that he was afraid to drink because he was a great sinner, and therefore unworthy of the water—that though others were welcome, he was not, because he was a great sinner. Would not the blessed man of God assure him that the water was as free for him as for any man in the camp? And is not the grace of Christ free for all sinners? If a man says he is afraid to come and drink because he is a great sinner, does not the Word assure him that he that cometh will in no wise be cast out—that if he be a great sinner, Christ is a great Saviour?

5. The rock gave its water to the children of Israel, not because they deserved it, but because they stood in need. The grace of Christ is offered to sinners, not on account of his own merits, but by way of a free gift. Would not any person that reads the history of the children of Israel suppose that people were ridiculing them if they said it was for their good deeds that they obtained water from the rock? But if a person reads the history of mankind in general, will he say that such-and-such characters merit anything at the hand of God? What merit has a beggar for stretching his hand to receive alms? Or what merit has a traitor for accepting a pardon from his prince? If the people of a whole province should rise in rebellion against their king and lawful governors, can that same people, after they are conquered, plead any merit because they are not so deeply guilty as their leaders?

The gospel addresses us as sinners because we are such. It offers pardon to sinners, to rebels of every denomination [designation]. It does not suppose any sinner upon the face of the earth to be innocent so as not to stand in need of its assistance. The language of our merit-mongers is this: 'God, we thank thee that we are not as other men—we are not such gross sinners as the adulterer and the extortioner. Others may talk of the deceitfulness of sin, and the danger arising from original and actual corruption. But we have not such a measure of it as to stand in need of the gospel. We live a decent life; we pay our debts and are good neighbours. We stand at an equal distance from the devotion of the bigoted over-righteous enthusiast, and the scandalous irregularities of the libertine. We do not choose to examine our consciences by the Word of God, for fear religion would put us mad, but we hope to go to heaven before any canting hypocrite in the country.'

When these are the sentiments of people's heads, no wonder though they should not receive the gospel. The language of the poor Christian is, 'Lord, have mercy upon me, a sinner'. The law accuses him—a guilty conscience, unbelief, and the suggestions of his grand enemy magnify all his sins. But when his heart is ready to be overwhelmed, the gospel comes in to his relief. The blessings of the gospel are offered him, not because he deserves them—he is conscious he does not—but because he greatly needs them. He sees his need. He is in the wilderness, and must come to the Rock for water to quench his thirst. The nations around them were not distressed with thirst like the children of Israel—they got their water at an easy rate. The people of the world get their comforts often very easily. The people of God are brought into the wilderness—their souls are in distress— they get no comfort in any created enjoyment—they see their misery—they feel their distress. Nothing can relieve them but the gospel—the water must come out of the Rock for them. There are plenty of blessings and comforts in the gospel for them—they are free for their use—they are purchased by another. They do not buy them with their money, or merit them with their good deeds; they receive them as the free gift of God through the merits of Christ. Though we deserve the wrath and curse of God, the gospel is free for our acceptance. Christ and all his benefits are offered to sinners without money or price. If we see our need we may come, and all sinners have the free and large offer of the gospel.

6. The water of the rock followed them, not for a day or a year, but during their stay in the wilderness. The influences of grace follow the people of God till they come to glory.

That many persons may have the appearance of religion, and afterwards turn lukewarm and indifferent, and perhaps turn back to their lusts and idols, and even ridicule religion and religious people, is a truth that falls under our daily observation. But notwithstanding this, the foundation of God standeth sure. The comfort of the doctrine does not belong to those who would turn the grace of God into lasciviousness, but to true Christians who make it their daily prayer to God to give them grace to persevere to the end. The water followed the children of Israel in the wilderness, but upon their rebellion the precious blessing was withheld till Moses strikes the rock a second time. The comfort of grace may be withheld from such of the people of God as fall into sin, till they renew their repentance and take hold by faith of the Saviour. We read in the Scriptures of several of the saints who fell into very great sins, but they did not entirely fall away for they renewed their repentance—they humbled themselves before God and were received into favour. This is very comfortable doctrine to the Lord's people, and it cannot be a pillow for carnal security to any man.

To the man who would reason in this foolish manner, 'I am now in a state of grace. I may indulge my lusts for I cannot fall away,' we would answer in the words of Scripture, 'Thou hast no part in this matter, for thy heart is not right before God; thou art in the gall of bitterness and bond of iniquity.' It is not the fault of the precious doctrine that sinners abuse it to their own destruction; other doctrines are abused as well as this.

Instead of disputing about it, let it be the business of our lives to secure the grace of God to our souls, to improve our talents and opportunities, and to go from strength to strength till we arrive safely at Zion. If a man is sincere, I believe he will persevere to the end. If a man once believes in his soul that the grace of God is more precious than created enjoyment, that the joys of heaven are more substantial than the joys of sense, nothing will stop his progress. Do we not see the wonderful effect that avarice and ambition have upon the human mind? And if the love of money, the love of praise, and the gratification of a lust, hurry people forward so that nothing can stop their career [headlong progress], is it to be supposed that the love of grace, the love of Christ, and the love of heaven can have less effect? Whatever is a man's darling object, he pursues it with perseverance. And when grace gives a new turn to the thoughts, grace follows the soul, as the water of the rock followed the children of Israel, till he safely lands in the heavenly Canaan.

3. Obtaining refreshing streams for our souls

As the rock did not yield water till it was struck, in like manner we must strike the Rock of our salvation, that we may obtain refreshing streams for our souls.

The mean [way] by which the wisdom of God saw fit to relieve the thirst of the Israelites was that the rock should be struck in order to supply them with water. It was an unlikely mean, and therefore it was greatly calculated to humble them and bring them to a dependence upon God Almighty alone. They were in great distress, but man's extremity is God's opportunity. We may believe that Moses, as well as the children of Israel, had murmuring thoughts—some secret unbelief, mixed with their faith. But their unbelief did not hinder the precious blessing from flowing to them. We may naturally think that they were in some measure at least brought to submit to the will of God before they could obtain their request. The water was to flow from the rock, and the rock must be struck.

We must likewise obtain the water of life by striking the Rock of our salvation. If such an expression may be allowed, God had no difficulty in bringing water out of the rock; the great difficulty was in bringing the people to submit to such a dispensation. There is mercy with God, there is grace in the Saviour, and there should be no difficulty in believing so. But the difficulty is in bringing the proud heart of a sinner to sue [appeal] for this grace as he ought.

The Rock must be struck before the water can be obtained. Moses struck the rock with the rod—we must strike the Rock by the exercise of faith and repentance. We ought to endeavour to believe that we shall obtain our requests. He permits us to use arguments with him, as if he were a man: 'Take with you words,' says he. Blessed Job says, 'O that I knew where to find him, and I would fill my mouth with arguments.' God is unchangeable, and our prayers cannot change his purpose or alter his decree. Prayer is the blessed mean by which he brings about his gracious purposes towards his people. In Scripture we see the greatest works performed in favour of his people by faith and prayer. Prayer is only faith expressed in words. As the heat and attraction of the sun raises vapours and melts the clouds into softening showers of rain, prayer, as it were, brings faith to perform general and particular acts of believing. It is not the strength of the child that opens the door of his father's house, it is the cry of the child that moves the father's heart to open—it is not his arguments, but the parental feelings, that open the door. He allows him to cry because he delights to hear his voice.

I shall mention some of the arguments which poor sinners may use, as these are the strokes by which they bring water out of the Rock.

1. God sent his Son into the world to save sinners.

We may put the Saviour in mind of his office. His business into the world was to destroy the works of the devil. This work is sin and unbelief—the work of God is faith and holiness. As faith or unbelief prevail, grace or sin will prevail also. Unbelief suggests to the sinner that he has committed such-and-such sins; faith goes with these very sins to the Saviour for pardon and grace. If we were to stand at a distance from the Saviour because we are sinners, who then could be saved? Instead of this, we ought to go to him as we are, for Saviour and sinner are relative terms. Our being sinners is what makes the Saviour precious to us. He came not to call the righteous, but sinners to repentance.

2. He has saved very great sinners, hardened sinners, that have continued long in sin.

Unbelief may go a step farther than to tell us that we are sinners. We may be great sinners, and some of the people of God, before their conversion, may have continued long in sin. The conscience may be seared, the heart hard, the will stubborn, the mind blind, and the feelings blunt. He may complain of being past feeling. But the Word assures us that all manner of sin shall be forgiven, and that the blood of Christ cleanses from all sin.

We have instances in Scripture of very great sinners that were pardoned and cleansed. And faith may plead this argument, that Christ is not only the Saviour of sinners, but the Saviour of great sinners. He not only can cure the spiritual palsy, but he can raise Lazarus out of the grave of sin in which he has been rotting, not for days, but for years. Is this an imaginary case? I appeal to history and experience. Such trophies of divine grace may encourage poor sinners to plead with the Saviour to have mercy upon themselves. Are we sinners? Are we great sinners? And have we continued long in sin? Such were Paul, Manasseh, the people of Corinth, and the murderers of Christ. The argument of the psalmist is, 'Pardon mine iniquity, for it is great.' Let us acknowledge that our sins are great, but let us plead that we have a great Saviour, able and willing to save to the uttermost all that come unto him. If our sins are heinous and highly aggravated, and our unbelief great in proportion, let us plead with him that he was not only wounded for our sins, and bruised for our iniquities, but that his precious side was pierced—that he encourages us in his gospel to thrust our hands in his side, and be not faithless, but believing—that by saving great sinners he will show his almighty power as a Saviour. Let us plead this argument.

3. As we stayed from him so long that we now have nothing to plead by way of merit, but we plead his own righteousness.

The language of our hearts sometimes is that if we had come sooner he would receive us. This thought, however, arises from a desire to be justified by our self-righteousness. There is one way of justification for all, namely, by the righteousness of Christ imputed to us. If we have been great sinners, this must be our plea—at any rate, we must make mention of his righteousness, of his only. Salvation is of grace. And whatever false opinions several people may have when they examine their sins—not by the law of God, but by their own self-love and the maxims of the world around them—we must acknowledge ourselves to be sinners and to stand in need of a Saviour. We cannot pretend to extenuate our sins—conscience and the Word of God give a different account of them. Are we sinners? He is the Saviour! Are we foul? He is the Fountain! Are we in debt? He is the Surety! We cannot pay our debt, or answer for one of a thousand of our transgressions, but he is the propitiation, and we plead this great sacrifice. And though Lebanon is not sufficient to burn, and the beasts upon a thousand hills are not sufficient for a burnt-offering, 'the Lamb of God taketh away the sin of the world'. We might formerly believe that our own endeavours, our prayers, our alms, and our duties might recommend us to God. But now, with the poor publican, we cry, 'Lord, have mercy upon us sinners!' We disclaim everything but what the Lord Jesus Christ has done and suffered, and that we build our hope upon him as the Rock of ages—that we beg of himself to bring us from every false foundation, to trust in himself alone as the author of salvation to our souls—that we desire to be found in him, not having our own righteousness, which is of the law, but the righteousness which is of God by faith.

4. He will get more glory by saving us than by destroying us.

God will be glorified in the condemnation or salvation of all men. He delights in mercy. The salvation of one soul brings more glory to him than the condemnation of thousands. Salvation is the work of God; misery and destruction is what men bring upon themselves by sin. People can destroy, but cannot save themselves. Misery is the work of men; grace and salvation the work of God. We may tell the Saviour that our everlasting happiness will procure glory to his name, for all the ransomed of the Lord are jewels in his crown, and will reflect honour upon him for ever—that the hosannas and hallelujahs of his people will be a greater pleasure to him than the groans and miseries of his enemies who smart under the hand of his justice.

5. If he will, he can save, and we may throw ourselves at his feet to do with us what he pleases.

We are sinners and, as such, we stand in need of a Saviour. The great work of grace is to humble the soul and bring the sinner, weary and heavy laden, to Christ. We are to receive comfort in the lowest posture of humility and resignation. We deserve nothing, and God is not obliged to give us any good thing unless he chooses of his own good pleasure—anything he does is of free grace. Though he would condemn us, we cannot complain. And therefore let us tell the Saviour that we throw ourselves upon the mercy of God through his merits, and entirely resign ourselves to his will—that though he would destroy us, we adore his justice, and receive the stroke with resignation—we are sinners, and his justice would be clear—that we throw ourselves upon his mercy, for he is a gracious God— that we have murdered our souls, but that we lay hold upon the horns of the altar—that though Solomon put Joab to death at the altar, he is greater than Solomon, and a king of greater mercy—that though the crimes of Joab were too great for Solomon to pardon, our sins are not so great but his blood can wash away their filth and their guilt—that though we tremble at his justice, we have some humble hope in his mercy—and if he would pardon our sins, gratitude would make us to devote our souls and bodies to his service.

6. Instead of a soft heart, we feel our hearts hard—instead of love to God, we feel enmity—instead of genuine gratitude, we feel selfishness. But he is God, and can cure us—he is our Physician, and we can tell him our diseases.

Sin is an awful disease, and such as felt it will acknowledge that it is so of a truth. A proud self-righteous person would be affronted to suspect his own heart was hard, that he had enmity to what was good, and that he could be capable of ingratitude to the best of beings. But what is the good of concealing our disease? Till we feel our disease, how can we apply for a cure? If a patient cannot bear to be told that his case is so bad that a physician is necessary, or, after applying to the physician, if he conceal from him his most secret and most dangerous wounds, can it be expected that he will cure him? The Saviour would cure us if we would apply to him—but either pride on the one hand, or unbelief on the other, hinder us from looking to our hearts and lives.

Many of us are like a man who had a deep and dangerous wound in the side, and a small cut in the finger. He shows his finger to the doctor, but conceals the wound that affected his life. When asked the reason of such foolish conduct, he replies that such-and-such a man applied a plaster to it. Besides, he was afraid the doctor would ask a high fee and oblige him to observe a strict and regular diet. But when the wound begins to pain him and threatens his life, he must show it to the physician.

Such is our case. We ask pardon for what we think small sins—we say nothing to him about our hearts and the great sin of our nature. We are afraid of mortification and self-denial, but when we feel our pain and see our misery, we must go to the

Saviour—we must tell him our disease, be it never so deep or so desperate, for there is balm in Gilead, and a physician there. Do we complain that we are dead in sin, without spiritual feeling? 'He is the resurrection and the life.' He can raise the dead sinner out of the grave, and give him life and light and joy. Let us tell him our case and pour our souls into his bosom—let us tell him that his healing hand can cure us—that we are afraid to look at the wound because unbelief says it is incurable—that we beg of our Physician to look at it himself, to see if ever the like of it came under his hand before, and though this should be the case, that he is not like other physicians—that we hope he will undertake our cure—that we believe it would not defy his skill or his power to heal our disease—that we pray him to handle our wounds, for his healing medicines can cure every disease— that we will not believe a bad report of him—that he can blot out our iniquities for his own sake, and that his blood can cleanse us from all sin.

7. Lastly, as he took our nature upon him, we may speak to him as our elder brother—that we appeal to his tender heart and feelings—that we are determined to thank and bless him whatever he does with us—that we shall wait upon him in the use of means, till he comes with his salvation to our souls.

Let unbelief, let the enemies of our souls, do their utmost; the worst they can say is, that God will destroy us at last. Let us complain of them to the Saviour—let us tell him we are determined to bless him, to seek him, and to serve him, as well as we can—that we watch at his gate, knock at his door, and wait his gracious time—and that, though he would frown upon us, the language of our heart is, 'The blessing of our souls upon his precious head, through all eternity'—that we deliver up our lusts and our idols, and beg of himself to open up the door of our hearts, that the King of glory may come in—that we are resolved to follow him—that his people shall be our people, and his God our God—that we shall run after him in the use of all means, attend at the pool of ordinances, and go where we think he shall be passing by. And thus, though we cannot change God, prayer may gradually change our own hearts. When Moses conquered his unbelief so far as to strike the rock, the rock gave water to the congregation—and Christ, the Rock of salvation, shall give water of comfort to our souls.

Inferences

1. As the children of Israel drank of the rock, but many of them did not understand the spiritual meaning of it, Christians may have the ordinances, and not experience their power. Water is a great temporal blessing. Every bad man, however, among the children of Israel had not the blessing or thing signified by the rock. Means and ordinances are a great blessing also, and they are valuable even for their temporal advantage to society. But the wicked do not reap any spiritual benefit from them. The gospel is hid to them, and this consideration should make us earnestly beg of God to reveal Christ to our souls.

2. Instead of boasting of our privileges, we should make a good use of them—they cannot save. The Israelites enjoyed astonishing privileges: God wrought wonderful things for them in the field of Zoan, at the Red Sea, and in the wilderness. The greater their privileges were, so much greater were their punishments when they made a bad use of them. It was not to encourage them in sin that they were privileged so highly, but to make them 'a peculiar people, zealous of good works'. Our

privileges, as Christians, should make us holy in life and conversation. Let us not rest satisfied with eating and drinking in the presence of our Saviour, and wearing his livery by an outward profession, but let us seek an interest in his love, and pray to God to engrave his image upon our hearts.

3. Lastly, a poor soul may say, I have often struck the Rock, but do not fetch water. Why? Unbelief is the cause. Unbelief made blessed Moses strike the rock twice, and speak unadvisedly with his lips. It is your duty to believe that you shall obtain your request. You cannot believe, but as faith is God's command and your duty, you should attempt it. The people present when Lazarus was raised from the dead, in spite of unbelief, could remove the stone from the grave. They did so, and the miracle was wrought. You have attempted to believe, but do not bring water out of the Rock. If you have not, you must strike the Rock over and over again. Continue to strike the Rock. It was the power of God, and not the rod of Moses, that wrought the miracle. It is not your striking that brings water out of the Rock. It is the favour and good will of God that brings comfort to our souls. We deserve nothing, and therefore we should wait patiently till God gives his gracious answer.

May God bless his word to our souls, and to his name be the glory, through Christ Jesus! Amen.

Sermon 2

The mountain of the Lord

And in this mountain shall the Lord of hosts make unto all people a feast of fat things, a feast of wines on the lees, of fat things full of marrow, of wines on the lees well refined. And he will destroy in this mountain the face of the covering cast over all people, and the vail that is spread over all nations.
Isaiah 25:6–7

AS there is no news so interesting to the people of God as the gospel, the prophets very often introduce it among other things. And as they delight in the subject in general, they look forward with peculiar pleasure to the more glorious days of the gospel—to the days in which all nations, Jews and Gentiles, shall make up the Church of God. After the prophet had given an account of the destruction of the enemies of the Church, he gives us a description of the feast of the gospel.

It was customary with great conquerors after subduing their enemies to make a feast for their friends. Thus we read of the feast of Ahasuerus. When the Saviour conquered his own and our spiritual enemies, he ordered the gospel to be published as a feast for all nations.

1. I shall attempt to give you a description of the gospel feast.

2. Where it shall be made.

3. For whom it shall be prepared.

4. The manner in which God shall prepare the nations for the gospel feast.

5. Lastly. Application of the doctrine.

1. A description of the gospel feast

I shall attempt to give you a description of the gospel feast. The greatest feast we read of in Scripture is the feast of Ahasuerus, which lasted one hundred and eighty days. There was first a general feast for all the great men of Media and Persia, and then a particular feast for the people of Shushan, the palace, which lasted for seven days, where the king gave several proofs of his glorious majesty.

In like manner, the gospel is a feast for all nations. There will be a general feast for all the Gentiles, and a particular feast for the Jews, after they are converted to the faith of Christ. At a feast there is great plenty of food—joy and delight of every kind.

1. The gospel is a feast because of its complete perfection and suitableness to every sinner's case.

In order to take a view of the gospel, let us take a view of sin, and, for this purpose, let us meditate for a little upon the fallen angels. Behold here the fatal effects of sin! Scripture informs us that the angels who kept not their first estate are reserved in chains till the judgment of the great day. The holy angels saw Lucifer, son of the morning, with all the accomplices of his guilt, shorn of their beams, and instead of their being stars of light, are now become dark globes, black and wandering stars, to whom is reserved the blackness of darkness for ever. What must therefore be their astonishment when they heard of the rebellion of our first father! They saw the effects of sin in superior beings, and it was natural for them to expect that mankind would share the same fate. With what joy and astonishment, therefore, did they hear the gospel news that man was to be redeemed—that the Son of God, in the fulness of time, would become man! Sin is an awful and filthy disease, but the gospel is in every respect a suitable remedy.

At a feast, as there are persons of different tastes, there are different dishes. The doctrine that may refresh the soul of one may be dry to another. But there are many great and precious promises in the Word. Some have strong corruptions, some have strong unbelief, strong temptations, and strong fears. Some have sickly stomachs, that they cannot taste any dish. These require cordials to give them an appetite. And as there are many dishes at this feast, there is what suits every man's taste. The landlord asks his guests what they would choose. One chooses one food, another a different. One wishes a pardon, another longs for comfort, and a third prays for strength. There is not a temptation, there is not a thought, there is not a doubt that can possibly rise in the mind, but there is some suitable word in the Scripture calculated to give comfort. One poor sinner looks upon himself as a nonesuch [a person without an equal]—a great, a very great sinner. The Saviour addresses him as he addressed his doubting apostle, 'Thrust thy hand in my side, and be not faithless, but believing.' Another may have knowledge—

he hears the gospel, he has no doubt of the Saviour's power—but is afraid he is not willing to save him—if he is saved, he thinketh it is by a miracle of grace. Even miracles of grace are promised in the promises of the gospel. Isaiah 43:19: 'I will do a new thing. I will make a way in the wilderness, and rivers in the desert.' The gospel is a complete feast, as it offers pardon to the guilty, grace to the unworthy, and strength to the weak.

(1) The gospel offers pardon to the guilty. The Lord Jesus came into the world to save sinners; he procured gifts for the rebellious, and is now exalted, a Prince and Saviour, to give repentance and pardon to the children of Israel. The declaration of Scripture is: 'Though your sins were as scarlet, they shall be white as snow.' Are we sinners? Yes—we are all sinners, and come short of the glory of God, and some of us are great sinners. The Saviour is held forth as an asylum or sanctuary for the guilty to flee unto. He is our city of refuge. Very guilty criminals could have no access to the cities of refuge; but the greatest sinners are welcome to Christ.

When our Saviour was upon earth, he did not complain that there were any sinners so great that he could not pardon, or their disease so desperate that he could not cure. The only class of sinners he excludes is those who refuse the remedy offered them with expressions of hatred and contempt, and properly speaking, they only exclude themselves. Though many of the Jews were very great sinners, the Saviour's great complaint of them is, 'And ye will not come to me that ye may have life.' He tells them, if they would not believe in him, they would die in their sins. The gospel does not exclude the guilty. The gospel calls the guilty. The gospel encourages the guilty sinner to come to the Saviour. The language of the gospel is this: 'Guilty sinners, why do you run away from Christ?' If you knew the tender feelings of his heart you would run to him. If you look on yourself as a very great sinner, you wrong the Saviour if you think him not a complete Saviour. He can blot out all your transgressions as a thick cloud, and as a cloud your sins. Look to the heavens above you and to the earth beneath you! It requires an exertion of almighty power to create a single grain of sand— an exertion of the same power can with the same ease create a universe. Had the Saviour more difficulty in raising Lazarus from the dead than in raising the ruler's daughter? Or had he greater difficulty in pardoning the sins of Manasseh than in saying to the man sick of the palsy, 'Thy sins be forgiven thee'? He had not. With the same ease he can pardon all sins. Are there any guilty criminals here? Come and welcome to the Saviour! The gospel is a feast, and here is your dish.

(2) The gospel offers grace to the unworthy. People who have not fallen into very gross sins, may perhaps think they have a claim upon the gospel. In this, however, they are mistaken, for it is not because we are worthy, but because we are unworthy that the blessings of the gospel are offered. No sinner is worthy, though some are more unworthy than others. There are a few of mankind who have not fallen into what the world calls gross sins, but when they get a view of the spirituality of the divine law, they will see themselves unworthy in the sight of God. An actual breach of any one of the ten commandments is a gross sin—and if this be true, as it certainly is, the generality of mankind have fallen into gross sins—and several of them have fallen into very gross sins. To all these unworthy sinners, the gospel comes with an offer of grace.

Such as have no money are invited to buy wine and milk without money and without price. You must obtain grace freely, or for some equivalent price. But what price can a sinner give for grace? Let us examine. Why, perhaps he gives a deal in charity to the poor. But, my friends, consider how precious is the grace of God—it is the divine image upon the soul. Should the king, who is the greatest man in the nation, expend a great quantity of money in the course of forty or fifty years upon several poor objects—could this procure grace for his soul? Can all the money in the world take away one sin? Can a scheme of duties and several devotional exercises take away guilt or procure the favour of God? Nothing can do this but the merits of Christ. The Saviour died to procure us the grace of God. We are not to pay anything for it, but to accept of it with thankfulness, and believe in the divine person that procured it for us.

That we are unworthy sinners, every part of the book of God clearly evinces, either in plain language or by plain and necessary consequence. But until we believe that we are unworthy, we cannot believe or prize the gospel. The Scripture says that all have sinned and come short of the glory of God. There are two arguments that prove who are unworthy sinners when other arguments fail. Many persons who think well of themselves and cannot be convinced that they are unworthy, have very different views when they turn dangerously sick or come to the point of death. In these awful moments they are as much afraid as your gross sinners—a proof that they are unworthy. Sickness or death did not make them unworthy, but only convinced them that they were so.

If we give ear to the Word of God and the voice of conscience they both declare us unworthy. Every mouth must be stopped, and every sinner plead guilty before God. If a number of people should rise in rebellion against their lawful sovereign, and one or more of them should plead that the stone with which he struck the king was not bigger than an egg, that it did not much hurt his majesty, would this argument be sustained? Would not the jury bring him in guilty? Would not the judge condemn him? Will not every person acknowledge that he is an unworthy rebel? And if the king pardons him, does not this proceed from his royal clemency, and not from his worthiness?

But if this same rebel, instead of imploring mercy, always insisted that many were more guilty than he was—that the stone he took up and threw at the king as he was passing in his carriage was but small—that the stone did not kill him—that he only meant to frighten the king—would not such defences prove that he was still a perverse rebel? Every sin against God is an attack upon his heavenly majesty. It strikes at his authority. And when we see our sins, instead of excusing them, or saying we are not so deep in guilt as others, we shall then take shame to ourselves, acknowledge our unworthiness, and throw ourselves upon the mercy of God, revealed to us in the gospel of our Lord Jesus Christ. For Christ is offered to the unworthy.

(3) The gospel offers strength to the weak. Christ is offered not only to sinners in general, but to those who are entirely dead in sin and going on in a course of wickedness. Habitual sinners in particular have no strength to perform the duties of the law, and no relish to partake of the pleasures of the gospel. Are these then excluded? They are not—God has no pleasure in the death of the sinner. He offers them grace to repent, and his Spirit to

work repentance in their souls. His complaint is, 'And ye will not come to me, that ye might have life.' As we cannot quicken ourselves—he is the resurrection and the life—he is exalted a Prince and a Saviour to give repentance to the children of Israel, and the forgiveness of sin. Do we stand in need of grace to repent? The language of the Saviour is, 'Ask and ye shall receive,' and 'How much more will your heavenly Father give his Holy Spirit to them who ask him?' Experience can assure us that, without the grace of Christ, we can do nothing. Shall we then give room to sloth and idleness because we cannot convert ourselves? Shall we reason against our own souls? If nothing at all was in the power of man, unbelief would not be our sin. The paralytic man in the gospel could not stretch his arm, and yet the Saviour commands him to do so. He attempts the duty—he was healed. May we not follow the example? We are commanded to believe. We cannot believe or repent. What shall we do? This is our duty: it is the will of God. Let us then throw ourselves at his feet, acknowledge our weakness and insufficiency, and ask strength to do his will. Let us not give room to our natural enmity, and ask, 'Why does God require us to do what we have no strength to perform?'

If a man was fallen into a deep pit, and another passes by, sees him in that condition and offers his help; he desires him to arise and come out of that pit. He answers that he cannot. He reaches a rope to him and desires him to lay hold of it, and that he will draw him up. Would not the unfortunate traveller reason very wickedly and ungratefully, if he upbraided his benefactor that he desired him to come out of the dismal place he was in when he saw that he could not, with all his endeavours, extricate himself? Would he not succeed better by gratefully thanking his friend, and telling him that, though he was much indebted to him, and would thankfully follow his advice, but that his hand was so benumbed with cold and weakness that he could not hold the rope? Will he leave him in this condition? By no means! He sends down a person to bind the rope about him, and then draws him up. Let us own our weakness, and that we cannot lay hold of the promise let down for our help. When the poor creature is in that weak condition, the Holy Ghost ties the promise about him and draws him up.

Are we dead without feeling? He is the resurrection and the life. He can breathe upon our dead souls and command us to live and come up out of our graves. If we find ourselves in a weak and impenitent state, he promises the new heart, and makes it our duty to pray for it, as he tells us he will be inquired of by the house of Israel to do it for them.

To say or suppose that wicked persons and people without grace are not commanded and encouraged to pray is to say that graceless persons are not commanded and encouraged to repent. The weak are those who have strong corruptions and no relish at all for holiness, and come such a length in sin as to laugh at religion. The wise man addressed such characters with a promise of the Holy Spirit to assist their weakness (Proverbs 1:22–23). In a word, guilty sinners, unworthy characters and persons destitute of all spiritual strength are encouraged to turn to God by the promises and privileges of the gospel. And when such characters feel their own situation, believe their danger, and apply to the Saviour for relief, these precious declarations of scripture are a rich feast to their souls.

2. Again, the gospel is a feast because of the universality of the gospel call.

The gospel is addressed to all indefinitely. It is a universal remedy, and offered to all that hear the call. If some great sinners were excepted, it would not be gospel then. None are excepted but such as except themselves. The most exceptionable characters are called—however aggravated their sins—however miserable their case—however poor their feelings. Sinners are called. Great sinners are called. Dead sinners without feeling are called. All sinners that hear the joyful sound are called. There is no clog upon the offer. If one in every ten thousand was excluded, the rest would be afraid such an offer would give a handle to unbelief. That the offer of grace is general is as clear as the sun in the firmament and we may answer every objection arising from unbelief, unworthiness, and want of feeling, in the words of our Saviour, in the words of comfort to those who endeavour to avail themselves of them: 'He that cometh unto me, I will in no wise cast out.'

You say you cannot come. I ask, 'Do you honestly make the attempt?' If you do, you need not be afraid but you will be welcome. If none had the offer but those who have the grace of God, how uncomfortable the doctrine! None could have comfort but those who are fully assured of their salvation. Our Saviour invited the weary and heavy laden, but he complains of others who had no feeling of the burden of sin, because they would not come. The gospel was to be preached to all nations— the first offer was made to the Jews as being the most guilty. However rich the feast at which a person is present, if he believes he is not welcome because he was not invited, he feels uneasy. But if the landlord says that all who choose to come are welcome, his scruple is removed. If a very great sinner, like the Jews of old, is afraid to come and that he is not welcome, scripture informs him that all that will may take the water of life freely, and, if sick of sin, all the ends of the earth are desired to look and be healed.

3. The gospel is a feast, because Christ crucified is exhibited to the view of our faith.

Pardon of sin is to be expected at the foot of the cross. As sure as bread and wine feed the body, a view by faith of the death and sufferings of Christ feeds, strengthens and invigorates the mind. Let us beg of God to give us this view of the tree of life, and we may then sit under his shadow with great delight, and his fruit will be sweet to our taste.

We are called upon to believe in the Redeemer and apply his merits to our souls. It is not enough to feed a person at a feast that he believes there is plenty of food on the table and that all are welcome to partake. He must reach his hand, take, and eat. We must feed upon Christ, take him as our own, and each must say, 'Christ is mine in particular.' We must not be content to believe that his death is sufficient for all—that he is offered to all that hear—but that he is offered to us in particular, and apply the balm of the blood to our own wounds.

We must make particular application of his death to our souls. Unbelief should not keep us back by suggesting to us that we are not broken in heart, and that it would be presumption to believe. Faith softens the heart. Is it presumption to come to Christ to get our hearts softened and our souls sanctified? He is exalted as a Prince and Saviour to give repentance and, as faith is the gift of God, we may ask it from him who procured gifts for rebels. The command of God is, 'Awake, thou that sleepest, arise from the dead, and Christ shall give thee light.'

Is it presumption in us to attempt to obey the command of God? At the time we feel ourselves dead, without the resentments of godly sorrow for sin. Our duty is to believe, that we may obtain the pardon of sin. And when God strengthens us to believe, a view of Christ crucified will effectually soften the heart with godly sorrow for sin. Let us then ascend the hill of Calvary, and behold the great friend of sinners stretched upon the cross. He died for sinners, and we may look. The brazen serpent was set up upon a pole for the benefit of the Israelites that were stung with the fiery serpents. It was not the feeling they had of their pain that c1520ured them. It was a sight of the serpent upon the pole. A sight of sin that would make us cry for pain cannot heal our souls. It is only a sight of our Saviour can do that. If we believed the efficacy of this cure we would certainly apply. Let us try. It is an infallible remedy—thousands have tried and were healed. This is the tree of life, and the leaves of the tree are for the healing of the nations.

4. The gospel is a feast on account of the comforts with which the souls of his people are refreshed.

The comforts of the gospel have often made the people of God forget everything else. They say with the disciples, 'It is good to be here.' Like the children of Israel at the bitter waters of Marah, when the wood of the tree of life is put in the waters, they are made sweet to them. The cross of Christ sanctifies their afflictions to them. When the Israelites pitched near Elim, it is probable it was one of the most comfortable stations [stopping places] they had during their stay in the wilderness. They had twelve wells of water, and seventy palm-trees. Sometimes the people of God meet with several springs of comfort in the wilderness. There are other times, however, when they get a

Pisgah view of the land of Canaan. Their joys do then abound. They have a heaven upon earth. A distant view of the spicy mountains [mountains of spices (Song 8:14)] raises their souls to heaven and, when they taste these sublime pleasures, they despise the pleasures of sin and sense. A draught of the river of life that proceeds from the throne of God fills and satisfies their souls. A day in the courts of God is better than a thousand. I appeal to the people of God. Is not one half hour of the pleasures of religion better than all the earthly pleasures that ever you tasted?

2. Where the feast shall be made

We are told it shall be 'in this mountain'. Zion hill was a type of the Church of Christ. The gospel sounded from Jerusalem to all the ends of the earth. What should hinder us to understand these words in the literal and spiritual meaning? We learn from Scripture that the destruction of Babylon has a literal and typical meaning, and we believe the comfortable promises respecting the hill of God have the same. And whether we understand the words of Jerusalem literally, or of the Church of God, in either case it will be fulfilled. The gospel will be a feast for all. It has been a feast for many of the nations of the earth already, and the time is coming when all nations shall hear the joyful sound.

The Jews shall have their large share of the feast. We read in the Acts of the Apostles that some of all nations under heaven were at Jerusalem at the time of Pentecost; and this was an earnest of the promise in the text. When the ancient people of God shall return to their own land, the fulness of the Gentiles shall come in to the Church. It is highly probable that people from all nations may visit Jerusalem, and in that case the promise in the text may be literally accomplished. It was from Jerusalem we got the gospel, which is, and will be, a feast for all nations.

The Church is compared to a mountain, because a mountain is conspicuous to all: a city set on a hill cannot be hid. The Church has been conspicuous at all times, in some sense or other. At the time her visible appearance has been most eclipsed, she has been conspicuous in another view. If a king builds a palace upon a mountain, it makes the outward appearance of it more beautiful, but does not add a whit to the height of the mountain more than if a peasant erects his cottage there. Whoever dwells upon a mountain will be seen, whether there be many or few. Whoever makes a profession to be truly religious will be taken notice of. Elijah complained that there was none to be seen upon the mount of God in Israel but himself. But though Elijah thought himself alone, he was not the less conspicuous.

In the latter days, we learn that many shall go up to the mount of the Lord; many shall seek the way to Zion with their faces thitherward. The Church may likewise be compared to a mountain because it is higher than other parts of the earth. When a person ascends a hill, he sees every other place below him. When we go up to the hill of God, we have place for meditation and retirement. We see the world below us. We commune with our hearts and open them to the Saviour, and thus prepare our souls for the feast of the gospel.

3. For whom the feast shall be prepared

The third thing proposed was, 'For whom this feast shall be prepared?'

The gospel is a feast for all nations. It is designed for all people, and in God's good time it will be exhibited to all. Sin is a universal disease. The gospel is a universal remedy. Physicians have never yet discovered anything that could be reckoned a universal cure. The gospel is a cure for every spiritual disease which sin has brought upon the soul. If it be so, some person may ask, 'Why was it not revealed to all nations? Why are not all who hear it saved?' Answer—If it was not sent to all comers, this has been owing partly to the negligence of the Church, partly to the wickedness of the heathens themselves. That the Church has been deficient of zeal in all ages is too obvious to require great proof. And as to the heathens, it is well known that, instead of embracing these glad tidings of great joy as they ought, they have often destroyed the persons who were sent with the joyful news to them.

As to the question, 'Why are not all who hear the gospel saved, if it be an infallible and universal cure?' Physicians who cure the body can assure us that they would infallibly save many lives from death if the patients would follow their prescriptions and apply the remedy. If the perverseness of some patients made them entirely refuse the remedy; if the intemperance of others prevented the cure from being effectual—in either case, the fault could not be imputed to the remedy or to the physician. With regard to the gospel, some obstinately reject it, and others content themselves by hearing it without applying the precious remedy to their souls. But there is balm in Gilead, and a Physician, whether sinners apply to him or not. He never refuses any that employ him, and the balm of his blood is freely offered to all without exception.

4. How God will prepare the nations for the gospel feast

The manner in which God will prepare the nations for the gospel feast—he will do this, the prophet informs us, by removing the veil and the covering. While there is a veil or covering upon a person's face he cannot perceive objects although they were near him. There is a veil upon the hearts of all men by nature that prevents their seeing their spiritual situation. There is a veil of ignorance, guilt and unbelief. It was usual for people to put a covering upon the face of a condemned person, that he might not see when he was led to execution. Mankind are in this situation. They are condemned criminals—there is a dark veil upon the eyes of their minds. They see not their danger, and where they are led. God promises to remove the veil, so that the criminals who were led forth to execution are admitted to the privileges of children and are made partakers of the gospel feast.

And this thick veil of ignorance, prejudice and guilt, is removed by knowledge, by preaching Christianity in its native simplicity, and by the influences of the Holy Spirit accompanying the preaching of the gospel.

(1) The veil is removed by the introduction of knowledge. Learning and knowledge pave the way for the introduction and reception of Christianity, by removing prejudices. Our holy religion made its first appearance at a time when mankind were enlightened with arts and sciences. The Lord Jesus Christ was born in the Augustan age [the age of Caesar Augustus]—an age famous for learning and learned men.

Learning and knowledge will qualify people for judging the arguments advanced in support of our holy faith. Accordingly we find that in all ages the most learned men, after going through the circles of the sciences, after enriching their minds with store of human learning, after making themselves masters of all classical knowledge, sat down at length at the feet of the prophets and apostles. Whatever respect we might have for the sages of antiquity, whatever relish as men of taste they might have for the beauties of the classics, they found the doctrines of salvation only in the scriptures of truth. They might find a great deal of human wisdom in the writings of antiquity, but they found the manifold wisdom of God in the redemption of sinners by the Lord Jesus Christ. Human knowledge, then, shall prepare the heathens for the reception of Christianity.

(2) Again, the veil will be removed by preaching Christianity in its native simplicity. In the purest and most orthodox churches, there are doctrines taught that are not necessary to salvation. The doctrines of the prophets and apostles are faith in a Redeemer, repentance unto life, and holiness of heart and conversation. These, and the doctrines more immediately connected with them, are the doctrines calculated to bring souls to a Saviour—Christ crucified is the great doctrine for poor guilty sinners.

(3) But, above all, the veil will be removed by the influences of the Holy Spirit accompanying the preaching of the gospel. Conversion to God is the work of the Spirit. It is the Spirit alone that can effectually remove the veil. In the first ages of the Church, preaching was attended with power. The gospel is preached in many places in the visible Church—no effects follow. They hear without concern. They even loathe the

manna; they have a relish for the flesh-pots of Egypt. It is manifest the veil remains upon their hearts. But when God's good time comes for converting the heathen and visiting his Church in mercy, the great Conqueror will gird his sword upon his thigh, and with his sharp arrows shall pierce the enemies of the King. Congregations shall not sit sleeping—the Word will come with power, and they shall take salvation to heart. When they shall see their misery by nature and practice, the glad tidings of the gospel will be a feast to their souls.

5. Application

1. Is the veil removed from your hearts? Did you see your danger by original and actual sin? Except you repent, you shall perish. The gospel can be no feast except you see your need of the heavenly manna. What is the language of your heart? Do you love the unsearchable riches of Christ, or the sordid pleasures of sin and sense, and the riches that perish? Is God or Mammon your portion? If you have no relish for the gospel, you can have no relish for heaven, and you cannot upon scripture grounds expect to be admitted to that holy place.

2. If you see your sin, come to this feast. You are welcome. If you complain you do not see your sin, beg of God to give you such a sight of it as will make you relish the gospel. To those who believe, Christ is precious. Pray to God to give you a sight of him that will satisfy your soul.

3. If you have been feeding at this feast, recommend it to others by your conversation and example. It is the duty of Christians as well as ministers to recommend Christ to sinners. Speak well of the Saviour, and take an opportunity to give a religious turn

when you are in company: say something—it may do good. By your example, live up to what you would recommend to others. People will not believe you if your lives belie your profession. If you are like themselves, how can you gain them to religion?

If you are under the necessity of humouring them in some things that are not sinful, take care to let them see you do so merely to do them good. People will humour children in order to make them learn. If we have been feeding with Christ in the ordinances, let people find the savour of good ointment about us, and this will induce them to come to the feast with us. Amen!

Sermon 3

The great and precious promises

Whereby are given unto us exceeding great and precious
promises: that by these ye might be partakers of the divine
nature, having escaped the pollution that is in the world,
through lust.
2 Peter 1:4

F AITH in the divine promises and in unseen objects is the
great support and consolation of all true Christians. The
happiness of the people of God is not in what they see—it
consists in promises. The happiness of children, even of great
men's children, consists not in what they presently possess but
in what their parents mean to do for them. Abraham and his
immediate successors are held up to our view as the great
example of faith. Now, their temporal or spiritual happiness in
this worlds did not consist in present possession. Palestine is
called the Land of Promise, a land flowing with milk and honey,
and it was promised to Abraham as a type of heaven. Now, the
children of Israel did not possess it for many years after the
promise was given. It was but a small part that Abraham himself

enjoyed of that pleasant country, and his posterity sojourned for several years in Egypt. But they had a promise of Canaan, and this was the joy and rejoicing of their hearts. Now, there is a heavenly Canaan promised to the children of God, and this is their joy and happiness. They have not much in possession, but they have their all in the divine promise. The children of this world may tell them as the son of a tenant said once to the son of a laird [estate owner], 'I have a better coat than you.' But the children of God may answer as the gentleman's child did, 'But my father is richer than your father.'

And what is the gospel but a promise of eternal life? And this life is in the Son. There is a heavenly Canaan promised, and if we can prove our relation to the Lord Jesus Christ, we have a title to it as sure as the descendants of Abraham, Isaac and Jacob could have to the earthly Canaan, owing to their relation to these holy men.

In speaking further upon these words, I shall point out to you:
1. Wherein consists the exceeding greatness and preciousness of the promises made to the people of God.
2. The character of the children of the promise—they are partakers of the divine nature.
3. The effect of embracing the promise—they escape the corruption that is in the world through lust.
4. Practical inferences.

1. The greatness and preciousness of the promises

I shall point out to you wherein consists the exceeding greatness and preciousness of the promises made to the people of God.

Things are reckoned great and precious among all men for their intrinsic value, as food and raiment, land and possession, and all the absolute necessaries of life. They are reckoned precious for the value set upon them, as gold, silver, and precious stones, and the favours we receive from near and dear friends and relations. And if the things that are necessary for this life are so very valuable, how precious are the things that are necessary for the spiritual and heavenly life! Now, the great things promised to the people of God, are:

1. A kingdom of glory in the life to come.

2. Grace to prepare them for the kingdom of heaven, and all needful spiritual supplies during their passage through this wilderness.

3. Such a competent portion of the good things and comforts of life temporal as the wisdom of God shall see meet for them—and these temporal good things are very precious, as they proceed from divine love, flow from the promises, and come to them through the precious channel of prayer.

In these three things consist the greatness and preciousness of all the divine promises.

1. There is a kingdom of glory promised to the people of God in the life to come, and this promise was made before the foundation of the world. Canaan was promised to the children of Israel long before they were born, and this, not for their own deservings, but because they were the children of faithful Abraham. And before we had a spiritual or even a natural being, grace is given us in Christ before the world began. We are chosen in Christ and obtain the kingdom, not because we deserve it, for we are sinners, but because he had made us his

people. There is a kingdom prepared for them—and our Lord tells us it was prepared for them from the foundation of the world.

They were chosen in Christ. Christ was chosen, and they were chosen with him to be his people. And, as they were chosen, there was prepared for them a kingdom they were to inherit. When God prepared a kingdom, he surely knew the people for whom it was prepared. He tells them at the day of judgment, in plain language, it was prepared for them.

And as it was prepared from the foundation of the world, it was not for any merit he saw in them, for they were sinners. He did not prepare it because he saw they were friends, for Scripture says they were enemies, and that he died for such. When a great man marries, he makes a provision for all his children, and for some of them perhaps before they have a being. But a great man cannot know whether he will have children or what number he may have. This cannot be said concerning God, for he surely knew all his spiritual seed for whom he was preparing the kingdom. They could not certainly convert themselves, or give themselves a spiritual birth. And if a man believes anything at all, he must believe that God knew beforehand whom he meant to convert, sanctify, and save—and consequently he knew for whom he was preparing this kingdom. There is a kingdom then promised and prepared for all the elect of God, and as there is a kingdom promised and prepared,

2. There is grace promised to prepare them for the kingdom of heaven, and all needful spiritual supplies during their passage through this wilderness.

When God chose his people, he saw that they were sinners—that they were foul—that they were graceless. He purposed then to give them grace, and he gave them grace in Christ Jesus before the world began. Grace is the most precious thing in this world. It does not come by chance; a man obtains it in consequence of the divine purpose. Grace is the execution of the divine decree—the performance of the divine promise. All the grace necessary from their first call till they arrive safe in glory, is comprehended in the grace given in Christ Jesus, 2 Timothy 1:9, and it consists in the following things. It is promised they shall obtain:

(1) Quickening grace.
(2) Renewing and restoring grace.
(3) Strengthening and comforting grace.
(4) Persevering grace to the end of their journey.

(1) They shall obtain quickening grace.

The Redeemer shall see the travail of his soul in a numerous spiritual seed. His children shall be like the dew from the womb of the morning, adorned with all the beauty of holiness, and shining in the bright robes of their Redeemer's righteousness.

Our Lord informs us that all that the Father gives him shall come unto him. He quickens whom he will. Now, the first sign of quickening grace is a feeling of sin and a sight of need. When the spirit comes he will convince the world of sin. A person that has natural life will have feeling of heat and cold, hunger and thirst, and all the wants of the animal life. And when God quickens us we have a sense of our spiritual needs, and cry to him that can supply our wants. It is God that quickens those who were dead in trespasses and sins. And when he quickens he gives faith, and this faith, the gift of God, is given to all whom the Father gives him.

And as natural life has a feeling of its own wants, and will naturally suggest to us the things we are to do to supply them, the spiritual life does the same. The spirit that quickens convinces of sin—we see our filth and misery, and this excites a desire after deliverance from both. The gospel proposes a remedy—it shows us the atonement—pardon is procured by virtue of the Saviour's great sacrifice. When this is seen and believed, it purifies the heart. The heart is naturally foul, and as a putrid lake produces a number of disagreeable living creatures, the foul heart produces swarms of nauseous and unbelieving thoughts. In the gospel there is a fountain to wash in, and a river of life, and when a stream from this river passes through the heart, it cleanses the thoughts from sin. The nature of grace is to cleanse, to sanctify, to enlighten, as well as to save; and when it quickeneth the soul it also sanctifies the heart.

(2) There is a promise of renewing and restoring grace.

The language of God to his people when they fall, is this, 'Return, ye backsliding children, and I will heal your backslidings.' And again, 'I will heal their backslidings, I will love them freely.'

The royal psalmist acknowledges that God had restored his soul and led him in the paths of righteousness for his name's sake. Before Peter fell, our Lord informed him that Satan wished to sift him like wheat, but that he had prayed for him. The gospel is a declaration of glad tidings to perishing lost sinners in general. Now, the gospel had been weaker than the old covenant of works if there had not been a pardon upon record on the renewal of our repentance. Accordingly, we are desired to do our first works and return to our first love. Indeed, the language of Scripture upon this subject is very strong, 'O harlot, hear the word of the Lord,' and again, 'Though thou hast played the harlot with many lovers, yet return to me, saith the Lord.'

And if this was not the language of the gospel, we may well ask, 'Who then could be saved?' Which of us has not broken the covenant of our God? Have we not treacherously given that heart to the creature which belongeth to the Creator? And if the very best of us was asked the question, 'Have we not cause of fear if there was no promise of renewing and restoring grace? Have we not grieved the Spirit, hardened our own hearts, and benumbed our consciences with sin?' And if we must plead guilty to these charges, what would come of us if the gospel did not offer us pardon? If this doctrine was not true, the people of God were the most miserable objects upon the face of the earth. We acknowledge that they are greater sinners than others, for they sin not only against light and knowledge—which the wicked may do—but they sin against grace also. They have abused the grace of God, and grieved the Holy Spirit, and driven away his motions from their souls. Now, there is this addition to their guilt which is not in the sins of the wicked. And is there any promise for such? Yes, where sin has abounded, grace does much more abound. That Christ is offering restoring and renewing grace is clear from the description given us of the Church of Laodicea: 'They were wretched, and miserable, poor, blind, and naked.' And yet they are invited to buy gold tried in the fire, and white raiment, and eyesalve. The Saviour assures us that he loved that Church notwithstanding the misery of their spiritual condition. He invites them to renew their repentance, and that he will give them the consolation of his grace. And if we are in the same state, we have the same encouragement and promise.

(3) There is a promise of strengthening and comforting grace.

We are called with a holy calling; we are brought into a state of holiness and virtue; we have spiritual enemies, and we must fight against them. When the Israelites came out of Egypt, the surrounding nations looked upon them with a jealous eye, and they had several battles to fight before they got possession of the Promised Land. But they became impatient at last, and despaired of seeing the accomplishment of the promise.

Our spiritual enemies stand in our way. We have found the combat fierce, and it is no easy matter to fight against the world, flesh, and devil. Unbelief is ready to suggest awful things, and magnify the greatness of the danger and the many and insurmountable difficulties that lie in our way. Our carnal reason and our carnal friends, as well as our spiritual enemies, are a clog to our souls in the ways of God. But our Lord is the great captain of our salvation, and our high priest before the throne, so that we may plead for strength and grace in the tune of need. His grace shall be sufficient for us, and as our day, so shall our strength be, for he will not leave nor forsake us. When we pass through the fire and water we shall neither be burned nor drowned. And though we are no better than worms in our own sight, yet by divine strength we shall even thresh the mountains. Like our divine Master, we shall drink of the brook in our way, and the comforts of the Holy Ghost, through the promises of the gospel, shall strengthen our hearts and dispel our doubts. By keeping near the waters of the sanctuary our souls shall grow like the willows. And when at other times we are like a parched wilderness, the dews of his salvation shall descend upon our souls. These sweet influences shall refresh our hearts and invigorate us in the ways of God. And the grace that strengthens and comforts, also purifies the soul more and more, and the more holy we become, the more our comforts and strength will grow.

By waiting upon God he promises to strengthen our hearts. Now we require strengthening and comforting grace
(a) Against the attacks of infidelity and suggestions of unbelief.
(b) Against the strong corruptions of our own hearts.
(c) Against all outward temptations that surround us.

(a) We require strengthening and comforting grace against the attacks of infidelity and the suggestions of unbelief.

When the apostle mentions some that had denied a capital [principal] point in Christianity, he adds immediately, 'Nevertheless, the foundation of God standeth sure.' Though the word of God is immoveable as a rock, the scoffs of infidels and our sinful, carnal reason have a great influence over weak and unstable minds. There are deep and high mysteries in Christianity which our reason cannot fathom, and it may ask, with Nicodemus, 'How can these things be?' But if we believe nothing but what we can understand, we shall prove sceptics in philosophy as well as divinity. Reason tells us there is a God, and he existed from eternity. But can reason *understand* this? Nor can we understand many things that exist in the material world. It is grace, then, that strengthens us to believe the deep doctrines of revelation.

Our Lord tells us so when he says, 'Blessed art thou, Simon Barjona: for flesh and blood hath not revealed this to thee, but my Father who is in heaven.'

And, as we require strength against the attacks of infidelity, we require it against the suggesting of unbelief. When we speak of unbelief, we generally mean the thoughts that disturb us respecting our own personal interest in the promises and the truth of their accomplishment, and we certainly require grace for this—for no man can believe except it be given him. Nevertheless, we are required to believe and to apply the promises to ourselves. If faith is the gift of God, we are to prize his gift highly—ask it fervently from him and believe him sincerely when he says, ' Ask, and ye shall receive; seek, and ye shall find; knock, and it shall be opened to you.' And we are to wait at his footstool until we obtain our request.

(b) We require strengthening and comforting grace against the strong corruptions of our own hearts.

Where is the man, whether converted or unconverted, but has strong sinful propensities to struggle against? The apostle Paul was a chaste, regular, well-behaving man, and he cries, 'Wretched man that I am, who will deliver me from this body of death?' No doubt struggles, prayers and endeavours have their use, but we must acknowledge that nothing less than grace can subdue sin and change the nature and the heart. After all our endeavours we must come to the Saviour, and none but himself can cast out sin, and put spirit and life and comfort in our souls.

(c) We require strengthening and comforting grace against all the outward temptations that surround us.

Our hearts are like dry fuel—we may even add, like gunpowder—ready to take fire at every temptation that applies to our corruption. And these temptations and snares are many and various. We are equally exposed to them from friends and enemies, from our secular concerns, and even from the duties of religion.

We cannot suppose any state or any particular occasion that is not exposed to danger of one kind or other. A single word or a single glance may raise a flame which may cost many years and many prayers to quench and subdue. We see and hear with peril, we breathe an infected air, and we ought to carry an antidote about with us. People that must be among the sick often take something to prevent infection. Now, grace is what makes our souls strong against the infection of sin. Grace guards all the avenues. Job made a covenant with his eyes, and the psalmist prays to turn away his eyes from beholding vanity. Now there is a promise of strengthening grace, for, according to our day, so shall our strength be. His grace shall be sufficient for us, not only against the invisible attacks of our spiritual enemies, but also against all outward temptations to sin.

When people are faithful to the grace they received, and honestly wish to be kept from sin, there is no doubt but the providence and the grace of God will take care of them. This is clear in the instances of Joseph and David. Though the temptation of the former was strong, God took care of him because he trusted in him. David fell because, instead of praying against the temptation, he yielded and suffered himself to be overcome.

There is a promise of grace in the time of need, but it is when one can plead the promise that we can call it our own. There are many promises of support and assistance in Scripture. When we find our need of one of them and plead it as suitable to our case, we have an interest in it, and it is not our own until we receive it by faith. Are we attacked with inward unbelief and outward temptation to sin? Let us believe the promise, 'Fear not, worm Jacob, thou shalt thresh the mountains.'

Our great high priest knows the heart of such as are exposed to temptations. He was tempted himself, and he had a feeling for those who are tempted also. And if we honestly apply to him, and trust in him, he will give us grace to assist in the time of need.

(4) There is a promise of persevering grace.

It is God that begins the work, and it meets with opposition, not only from the human heart, but likewise from all the enemies of his glory, whether visible or invisible.

There is a formidable conspiracy against the least grace in the heart of any saint. And if God had not resolved and promised to carry on the work it must surely fail—where he has begun it, he will surely carry it on. Our Lord will not put it in the power of his enemies to scoff and say, 'This man began a spiritual building and could not finish it.' If there was not security in the promise for our perseverance, I do not believe that a single soul could be saved. And we might ask the greatest Christians upon earth what secured their standing. Is it the grace they possess, or the grace that is in Christ Jesus? There are some who make a better use of grace than others, but in the nature of things, grace will make people faithful, vigilant and honest. If people are not so, they may conclude they have not yet received grace.

If people seemingly devout afterwards fell away, it does not affect the doctrine of perseverance in the least. If they went out from us they were not of us. If people turn cold, and neglect means and ordinances, we may, without breach of charity, conclude they were not honest at first.

There are three things secure our perseverance:
  (a) The nature of grace
  (b) The promise of God
  (c) The prayers of his people.

(a) The nature of grace secures our perseverance.

It is like every other principle, it grows. Is it probable that an elegant scholar, who has made progress in science, will give up his pursuit and plunge in ignorance and barbarity? Is it probable, or even possible, that the man who has been often feasted with the food of angels all his days, would again plunge in the ditch and wallow in the mire? It is not.

(b) The promise of God secures our perseverance.

We may argue the perseverance of his people from the divine promise. He that has begun the work will finish it, for he will never leave nor forsake us. The soul is immortal, and it must live for ever. Now, grace is a divine principle—it has the

Holy Spirit for its author. If a parent will provide for the wellbeing of his child, we may conclude that God will secure the life of grace. It is his image on the soul; he loves his own image, and it is the object of his care.

It is true, Adam and the evil angels lost the divine image, but the causes are widely different. They stood upon the strength of the grace bestowed upon them at their creation, and there was no promise to secure their perseverance in holiness. Grace might die, and so might a human soul, if God had so pleased. Scripture says they will live for ever, and the soul that has grace will live happy for ever. Our Lord says, 'Because I live, ye shall live also.'

(c) Prayer secures our perseverance.

We may infer the doctrine of perseverance from the prayers of his people. Where is that Christian who does not make it his daily prayer to God to secure his perseverance in a state of grace? If he possesses such a treasure, he will be anxious to keep his possession. He will put up many ardent petitions to God to keep him from falling. He will give up the keeping of his soul to God, through Christ, as to a faithful Creator. He knows whom he has believed, and that he will keep what he has delivered to him against that day. If he has delivered his soul to God a thousand and a thousand times—if he has by faith repeatedly surrendered himself to his Redeemer, hoping to be saved by his blood and prepared for his heavenly kingdom—and if the promise and oath of God are security for such characters, we may safely conclude the perseverance of the people of God.

But what if such persons commit sin and fall from their duty? If they do so, the promise of God binds him to chasten them with rods—to hedge up their way—to bring them to the wilderness—to pursue them with awful providences or terrible temptations till they renew their repentance, and come again, weary and heavy laden, to Christ.

3. There is a promise of such a competent portion of the good things and comforts of life temporal, as the wisdom of God shall see meet for them.

And these temporal good things are very precious, as they proceed from divine love, flow from the promises, and come to them through the precious channel of prayers. Our Lord himself, in the prayer he taught his disciples, instructs them to pray for their daily bread. Temporal good things, when considered with the relation they have to spiritual things, are far from being small blessings. The Christian asks and receives them from God, and this makes them precious gifts.

If I receive a present from a poor man, I value it for the goodwill of the giver, but if I receive a present from the king, it would give me great pleasure and the world would reckon me happy. What makes the whole world, Christians as well as Jews, have such a value for the land of Canaan? It was because God gave it as a gift to the children of his friends, Abraham, Isaac and Jacob. If a man is a Christian, he gets his temporal blessings from God—they are a part of what is promised in the covenant, and they are consecrated by prayer. A piece of hard, dry, barley bread would be but poor food, but if that piece of bread is left steeping for a night in a vessel full of honey, it would be pleasant to the taste next day.

I was acquainted with a valuable woman that lived once in this parish. She was poor, but her poverty was sanctified. A young man came once into the house in which the old woman lived; she was eating a few potatoes, and had nothing with them. He observed that she had but poor food. She told him that she had kitchen [a condiment] with them which he did not see. When he wished to know what it was, she informed him it was Christ. Now, I can say with truth, that her few potatoes, without bread or butter or milk, were a most precious diet. A graceless worldling, with twenty dishes on his table, never had such a feast.

Let Christ be my portion and sanctify my worldly substance, and then I need not envy the riches or the possessions of those who seek their portion only in this life, and whose names are written in the earth. Worldly people may be surprised that Christians should ask temporal good things from God—and it is much to be lamented that too many of his people, by their practice, show that they deal too much in this doctrine. If they asked and received their temporal good things from God through prayer, they would not be so distracted with worldly cares as they often are. We find, however, that his people in Scripture asked their temporal blessings from himself—that they cost them prayer, and were the fruits of prayer and promises.

Riches, wives, and children, came to them through the channel of prayer, and they often acted faith upon the divine promises before they obtained them. The exaltation of Joseph, David, and Mordecai were temporal things, but when we consider the divine interpositions and astonishing providences and the ardent prayers that were engaged in their exaltation, we are led to confess that they were things of great consequence. The temporal and everlasting salvation of the people of God was promoted by these great events.

Marriage is a temporal thing. Isaac, the child of promise, got Rebecca from God by prayer—she proved a blessing to his family and a help to his soul. Ahab, the king of Israel, married Jezebel—she proved a curse to his family, and brought destruction upon his soul. Much depends upon temporal things, and they have a great connection with our everlasting state.

Solomon, the wisest of men, says (Proverbs 3:6), 'In all thy ways acknowledge him, and he shall direct thy paths.' There is not a temporal enjoyment but it is promised in some part or other of the Word. And why are they promised, but that his people may plead them and make them the subject of faith and prayer? When people cut and carve for themselves, they generally pay dear for following their own wisdom without consulting God. His people beg of him to choose their inheritance for them. He fixes their habitation, and makes a proper choice for them. He is providing a kingdom for them, and he will withhold nothing that is good for them during their minority.

2. The character of the children of promise

The character of the children of promise—they are partakers of the divine nature.

The promises of the gospel are let down to the earth to draw up our faith and love to heaven. By embracing the promises we become holy.

We never become partakers of holiness but in and through a promise. Now the children of the promise are partakers of the divine nature:
1. By their union with the Lord Jesus Christ.
2. By communion with God in prayer and ordinances.
3. By embracing Christ anew in every promise they plead, whether temporal or spiritual.

1. The children of the promise are partakers of the divine nature by virtue of their union with Christ.

That glorious person is offered in the gospel. The gospel is made up of promises. By receiving and welcoming the offer, we are united to him. Now that union is explained in Scripture by three strong similitudes: the union of man and wife—of the vine and branches—of the head and body.

We are united to the man Christ Jesus, and in and through him to God. He dwells in his people by his Spirit and by the virtues and graces of the Christian life. Now, this union is as sure and real as the union of the two natures in himself—the human and the divine. We cannot explain this union between Christ and his people, by which they become holy, though we know it really exists. This union makes us like to God as the wax is like the seal. They become one. They have one nature and holiness. They receive grace, and that grace proceeds from Christ. They have one interest. The husband and wife have one interest— whatever promotes the one, advances also the other. If the one is exalted, it reflects honour upon the other. The advancement of the Redeemer's kingdom is the joy—and, in fact, the advancement—of every individual that belongs to him. They are not complete, till the whole are brought in. And they have, in consequence of this, one will. 'Thy will be done' is the prayer of every one of them. As far as we pursue the will of God, and no further, are we real Christians? The great design of every dispensation is to make us acquiesce in, and submit to, the will of God. What belongs to Christ in us, will submit to the will of God; what is in us of sin, will rebel. And when we are entirely brought to his will, we shall be introduced to that kingdom where all the subjects do the will of the king.

2. They are partakers of the divine nature by communion with God in prayer and ordinances.

God speaks to his people in his Word, and they speak to him by faith and prayer. It was the Word that gave them a new nature at first, and it is the same Word that increases and cherishes this new nature in them. In all their wants, they are encouraged by promises. By believing promises, they honour God and promote their own comfort, and it is in this way that this communion is kept up. It is through a promise they receive Christ. This is the swaddling cloth in which the heavenly babe is always found, and when we receive him, there is always joy in such an act of faith. Old Simeon rejoiced when he had him in his arms, and it is only when we have him in our own arms that we can rejoice and have communion with God. Before Simeon had him in his arms, he often embraced him in his faith. He believed the promise, the great promise that contained him and which, like the river of paradise, was branched into other promises. And he is still in the promise; and when we embrace the promise, we receive Christ: and this is the way in which communion with God is begun and kept up. Prayer and ordinances are the channel through which we receive divine promises, and divine promises purify the heart and make us rejoice in God! Now, when the Spirit of God enables us to believe the promises, they become our own, we have an interest in them, and they rejoice our hearts.

3. They are partakers of the divine nature by embracing Christ anew in every promise they plead, whether temporal or spiritual.

The covenant of grace is a wonderful covenant. It contains everything we can wish or want. We have great duties to perform, and great wants to supply, and we have no strength for either. We are commanded to believe and to repent; by experience we find we cannot perform these duties. What will we do then? He promises a new heart (Ezekiel 36:25–26). 'He is exalted a Prince and Saviour, to give repentance and remission of sins' (Acts 5:31), and he says expressly, 'Ask, and ye shall receive' (Matthew 7:7), and again, 'I will be enquired of by the house of Israel to do it for them' (Ezekiel 36:7). There is no duty required without a correspondent promise.

We have also great wants to get supplied. Are we tossed with great unbelief because we are great sinners, and afraid to come lest we should not be welcome? Himself says, 'He that cometh unto me, I will in no wise cast out.' Are our sins deep? He says, 'They shall be white like snow.' Are we afraid to meddle with the promise, because we did not perform the condition, and do not find such-and-such qualifications? We are commanded to look to him that we may be saved. By receiving him we find qualifications, for all the promises are yea and Amen in him to the glory of God.

If we have great trials, he promises to support us. And if we are in such a state that we can see no promise that can belong to us, let us plead the great promise that he came to the world to save sinners. And if we do not see our spiritual needs, he is a great physician of souls, and can cure all diseases. Now, when we plead a promise, we are to receive Christ, and by believing a promise, it is our own—this will purify our hearts and fill them with joy and gratitude. If we go as poor beggars to the Saviour, and are content to live upon his bounty, this is the sure way to be rich, happy and wise. Let us seek Christ in the promise.

3. The effect of embracing the promise

The effect of embracing the promise—they escape the pollution that is in the world through lust.

Before the prodigal returned to his father's house, he longed for the husks the swine did eat, but after he was readmitted to his father's table, he did not envy them any longer.

The cause why people have such a relish for the pleasures of the world is that they do not taste the sweetness of the promises. Moses had it in his power to be called the son of Pharaoh's daughter, and enjoy the benefit of such adoption. He might enjoy the pleasures of sin for a season, but he saw more in the promises made to the people of God. Abraham, at the call of God, left the land of his nativity, and came to the land of Canaan to sojourn there. He received it in a promise as a type of heaven. He did not seek his ultimate happiness in the land of

Canaan, for he looked for a city which has foundations, whose builder and maker is God.

Now, what kept such holy men from plunging in all the irregularities they saw in the world around them? It arose from this, that they embraced the promises as their portion, and believed firmly in that future state of happiness which is reserved for the people of God. The world around them might look upon them as a set of well-meaning enthusiasts—the purity of their conduct and the holiness of their lives they could not call in question, but they would consider their happiness as rather visionary when they spoke of a kingdom and country to be enjoyed after death. They would consider Abraham, the father of the faithful, as a person who had a religious craze, when he made himself believe that an old woman who was long past childbearing would have a child, and the children to spring from this son were to inherit Canaan. His view of a future state, in their opinion, might be as ideal as the notion of his children by Sarah then possessing all the country from the Mediterranean to the river Euphrates. Their principle was, 'Let us eat and drink, for tomorrow we die,' and they acted accordingly. If people who have the benefit of revelation live like brutes, is it a surprise that blind heathens should abandon themselves to all sorts of debauchery? And what hinders the people of God from following the example of infidel Christians? They believe the promises, and by this escape the pollution of lust. The victory that overcomes the world is their faith—it shows them the glory of heaven, the grace and power of Christ, and the danger of yielding to the foe.

4. Practical inferences

From the doctrine we have heard arise the following practical inferences:

1. Though the promises belong to the people of God, and no other at the time can receive comfort from them, yet others are not excluded from believing and embracing them.

And this answers an objection that may arise in the heart of some of my hearers. You say that though these are great and precious, they do not belong to you, and you cannot plead because you have no grace, no faith. Permit me to ask you, 'Who told you that a man without grace had no right to believe, embrace or plead a promise?' Hear the Saviour himself (Isaiah 45:22), 'Look unto me and be ye saved, all the ends of the earth.' Had all the ends of the earth grace or faith? The apostle Peter tells the murderers of Christ (Acts 2:38–39) that 'the promise was to them and their children, and to all that were afar off, as many as the Lord our God shall call.' Now the call is to you.

You say you are far off, and have no right to the promises. The apostle tells us (Ephesians 2:17) that Christ preached peace to them that were far off. Believe the promises and you will be brought nigh. Are there no great and precious promises made to sinners? If you read Isaiah 49:8–9, you will find great promises to the Saviour about sinners. Are you then in prison or in darkness? Plead the promise. He came to seek and to save lost sinners, and his commandment to you is to believe. And what is faith but embracing and pleading a promise? Come as a sinner to Christ, and in him you shall find all the promises yea and amen.

2. Again, if we actually have, or earnestly wish to have an interest in the promises, their genuine effect is to produce holiness. And if this is true, we may conclude that those who live in sin are yet strangers to the gospel.

When our Saviour was upon earth his very touch, nay, his bare word, cured those who applied to him. When the blind and the lame showed the world that they could walk and see, this was proof enough that they applied to Christ for a cure. If the man who was once a sinner adorns the gospel by a good life and conversation, we may give him credit when he tells us that Christ cured his soul. The tree is known by its fruits, and purity is the genuine production of faith. Faith receives Christ, and if we receive him, he engraves his image upon our soul—and when we receive Christ we receive all the promises with him.

Some of the people of God may follow Christ in the dark. They attempt to believe and find the work difficult. But though they should be in bondage all their days through slavish fear, they are safe. Follow them to their retirements—they endeavour to believe and love Christ. Follow them to their secular concerns—they recommend him to others. They endeavour to believe and embrace the promises—they find they cannot—they cannot go further. They therefore leave the work in the hand of God—and though they are without comfort, the everlasting arms are under them and will secure their happiness. The Israelites at the Red Sea left the work to God and soon after did join in singing the song of Moses and Miriam. If we love the promises, our lives will be like the gospel.

3. Lastly, we may see here the advantages that accrue to us by embracing the promises.

(1) And in the first place by believing the promises we secure our everlasting happiness. Those who now are admitted to the joys of paradise (Hebrews 6:12) are said to inherit the promises. Canaan was promised to the Israelites, and they possessed the promises made to their fathers when they enjoyed that pleasant country.

Promises may be compared to charters and to banknotes. When a man receives Christ in the gospel promises, he has a charter for heaven. By embracing other promises, whether spiritual or temporal, we increase our heavenly riches, and we have this additional blessing and comfort, besides that we have a reading of our charter, and this strengthens us more and more. The more money we lay up in the royal bank of heaven, and the more promises we plead and believe, the greater is our stock. Earthly banks pay only simple interest, but though the Saviour sometimes delays his payment, he is sure to give compound interest at last.

(2) Another advantage arising from this trade of dealing in the promises is, that many of our prayers and divine promises which we thought were lost, dead, and buried, shall give us great joy in the accomplishment.

There are some merchants whose trade is so extensive that profit is poured in upon them by every wind that blows or is mentioned in the compass. Such, however, often sustain losses, and many of their vessels suffer shipwreck. Not so the Christian—his prayers are remembered, his tears are in God's bottle, and his cup of cold water shall be amply rewarded. His works of faith and labours of love shall be all registered and meet him with comfort. The promising God will be a performing God. If there is delay in accomplishing a promise, the Christian fares as Mordecai did—it shall be accomplished suddenly and unexpectedly. When God looks in his book he finds such a man pleading such a promise, and, waiting upon him and doing his duty, the answer will be precious and astonishing.

(3) To conclude, the more we believe the bare word of God's promise, the more we honour him and promote his glory. We know the story of the philosopher to whom Alexander gave an order to draw upon his treasurer. He drew a great sum. When the first of the present reigning family got a right to the crown of Great Britain, he gave promises and notes to several persons that applied for posts. One man applied, and was offered a note. He told his Majesty his royal word was enough. This pleased the king so much that he said he would get his suit [petition], whoever would be disappointed. Let us then make it the business of our lives to live upon the promises and follow the example of those who now inherit them. Prayer and promises feed faith, and faith supports the Christian life.

God bless his word! Amen.

Sermon 4

Tribulations of the people of God

And he said to me, These are they which came out of great tribulation, and have washed their robes, and made them white in the blood of the Lamb. Therefore are they before the throne of God, and serve him day and night in his temple: and he that sitteth on the throne shall dwell among them. They shall hunger no more, neither thirst any more; neither shall the sun light on them, nor any heat. For the Lamb which is in the midst of the throne shall feed them, and shall lead them unto living fountains of waters: and God shall wipe away all tears from their eyes. *Revelation 7:14–17*

T HIS book of Revelation is a prophecy of the things which were to happen to the church till the end of the world. And though the prophecies are dark and mystical, and cannot fully be explained in their utmost latitude until the providence of God unfolds their meaning, yet notwithstanding we can gather this much from them upon a bare reading, without overmuch study that, after a dark night of trouble, the Church is to enjoy very clear days of the gospel.

The Antichrist in the East shall be destroyed and the Jews, those princes of the East shall return to their own land. The angels which are bound in the river Euphrates are said to be prepared for an hour, a day, a month and a year. The waters of that great river shall be dried up. Whatever be the import [significance] of this, it would appear that the Antichrist in the West shall fall much about the same time with the Antichrist in the East. As the two Antichrists began, it is probable they will end alike. And when this great revolution will take place, the Church will enjoy the gospel ordinances in their purity.

We see there is a blessing promised to those who read, hear and obey the words of this prophecy—a proof that the Church can understand the general import of what it contains. Indeed, we who live in this last age have one advantage—that if we examine the history of the Christian Church, it is a commentary upon this book of Revelation. And when the providence of God shall develop his decrees, we shall clearly see what is the import [significance] of the whole book.

In the words just now read, we have an account of the sufferings of the people of God, and the state of happiness to which they will be introduced at last. In speaking further upon these words,

1. I shall mention some of the tribulations through which the people of God must pass before they enter into a state of rest and happiness.

2. The procuring cause and the means by which they are prepared for this blessed state.

3. The happiness or blessed state of the saints after death.

4. A word of improvement.

1. The tribulations of the people of God

I shall mention some of the tribulations through which the people of God must pass before they enter into a state of rest and happiness. As we are all sinners by the fall of Adam and our own apostasy, we must return to God by repentance, and this cannot happen without sufferings of one kind or another. It is a painful thing to go under the physician's knife, however tender his heart or his feelings may be; sometimes, however, it may happen that our health and preservation of our life may require this panful operation. Our spiritual Physician has a tender heart and a soft hand. Our diseases require, however, some sharp medicines to wean our affection from this transitory scene of things. If we were always in ease, we would make this our rest and our home. When we are in affliction we look up to heaven. Affliction teaches us to pray. When the Saviour was upon earth, who followed him? The poor, the miserable the blind, the lame, the distressed, the sick. The Saviour, in this respect, is like David. He becomes a captain over those that are in distress, those that are in debt, and those that are discontented, and come unto him for relief. Now, all the people of God come through great tribulation, and tribulation is made the happy means of bringing their souls to Christ.

John, it is very probable, had in his view in a particular manner the martyrs who suffered for Christ, but his words may be justly applied to all his followers. The tribulations through which they pass are:

1. Distress of mind arising from a sense of guilt.
2. Temptations to sin.
3. The trials of life.
4. Persecution on account of religion.

1. Distress of mind arising from a sense of guilt.

Distress of mind arising from a sense of guilt—a conviction of sin—a view of our transgressions in thought, word, and deed—will naturally produce fear and distress. Guilt is the parent of unbelief, unbelief creates fear, and fear hath torment. Though this fear and unbelief, properly speaking, is no part of repentance, yet it very often accompanies it, as we see smoke where there is fire. When a wound is dressed, and the rotten flesh is cut off by the surgeon's instrument, this cannot be without pain; but this pain is not the cure, though it accompanies it. Medicines often make the patient sick, and this is a symptom of their efficacy. However, we may say of repentance, this sickness is not unto death but for the glory of God and the good of the patient. When the Spirit of God gives a view of sin, this view will naturally produce terror, but that terror originally arises from sin. If a man should fall asleep upon the brink of a precipice, and his friend comes and awakens him, and gives him a view of his situation, and shows him that he was within a few feet of falling from the rock and being dashed in pieces, the terror that arises in him is not the fault of his friend—it must be imputed to his own misconduct.

The pain, the anxiety, the misery we feel, is often a natural concomitant of true repentance and it prepares our souls for Christ and for the consolations of his gospel. Something of this all the people of God are acquainted with at one time or other. Great sinners feel them in a great degree, and the most virtuous characters are not strangers to them. And what is still more astonishing in the economy of grace is that some of those whom the world call virtuous characters suffer more terrors before they come to Christ than very gross sinners. The cause, probably may be this: the gospel call is directed to all to come as miserable sinners and forlorn beggars to Christ, and that they shall be welcome. The great sinners see nothing in themselves that can recommend them—they are therefore sooner humbled, whereas the self-righteous are worse to convince of their need of a Saviour, and thus pride stands between them and the comforts of the gospel. From all these terrors the people of God are set free at death.

2. Temptations to sin.

Another source of tribulation is temptations to sin of various kinds.

The Saviour, though pure and undefiled, was tempted to sin, and for forty days together was exposed to the most violent onsets [assaults] of the wicked one. In his holy human nature there was no fuel for the temptation, but the tempter has many and various advantages over us. We have a body of sin, and he has plenty of matter to work upon. Our body is a clog to our soul. We oftentimes find it dull and heavy. We feel a great depression of the animal spirits and, what is worse, the constitutional sin makes the most furious struggle when the body is in disorder. The enemy takes the advantage of this, and then greatly plies his temptations. He loves to fish in troubled waters. And the people of God are more or less troubled with a body of death. And when they find the motions of sin very strong within them, comforts suspended and the Spirit withdrawn, they are apt to form desperate conclusions. This is the language of their experience, 'Hath God forgotten to be gracious? Hath he in anger shut up his mercy?' Zion hath said, 'The Lord hath forsaken me, and my Lord hath forgotten me.'

They find no love to God, and therefore foolishly think that he has no love to them; they find sin strong, and no relish for prayer or freedom in duty. This distresses them, because they think that God has forsaken and given up striving with them.

These distressing thoughts many of the people of God are acquainted with, and they arise partly from their inward corruptions, partly from the state of their bodies, and partly from their ignorance of God's dealing with his people. They sometimes think that the man of religion should be always full of joy, and get the complete mastery over his passions and appetites, and that a feeling of sin is inconsistent with anything that is good. But this is supposing earth to be heaven, and that we ought to triumph before we fight our battles. This is a state of warfare, and though we shall conquer at last, we cannot expect to escape without wounds. The struggle between flesh and spirit, between faith and unbelief, must be very painful. A person feels pain who has been long praying and gets no answer, who has been long struggling and gets no victory, who has been long waiting and gets no deliverance. And what adds to their distress is that they know it is their duty to recommend religion to others. When they do not find comfort in their souls, they find this very difficult. They are called upon, likewise, to rebuke sin. It is a distress to them to do this, when they find it strong in themselves, and conscience tells them so. From this struggle they are likewise set free at death.

3. The trials of life.

Another tribulation is the trials of life. There is no state without them. If the beggar feels the distress of poverty, let the question be asked at the rich, and they will confess that they possess only a splendid kind of misery.

The happiness of life has a load of misery and the people of God are not exempted from them—they have often a double share of them. Let us go where we will, we always hear complaints of some kind. Indeed, the half of our table conversation is very often complaint. Some complain of sickness, some complain of death, some complain of their friends, and others complain of their enemies. One man has a bad neighbour, another has a bad wife and a third has an unruly family. It is a mortifying speculation [spectacle] to a good-natured man that is obliged to be in several companies, that by far more than two-thirds of their discourse is nothing else than backbiting their own species.

We may pursue this speculation further. Let any person take up one of the public papers in his hand, and he will find that the most of the news is a history of the miseries of the human race, and this very often in the time of peace as well as in time of war. The most part of all history is an account of human misery or fear. All outward trouble may be reduced to these four: bodily pain, poverty, loss of friends, and disappointed hopes.

First, bodily pain. This is the greatest natural evil that can befall us. And who is not subject to it? One half hour of it will make us have no relish for any enjoyment under the sun. What pleasure can the richest man upon earth have when he feels an acute pain of the gout, though he should lie upon a bed of down, though the most exquisite dishes were presented to him, and though he should he charmed with the sweetest music? Pain will take away the sense of pleasure, and nothing can satisfy him till it be removed. Poverty is a distressing load. And as for the death of friends it is but losing a past of ourselves. It is sometimes like cutting off a right hand or plucking out a right eye.

Disappointed hopes are very distressing. We expect again, such or such a time, to see our friends and be happy with them—the next news we hear is their death. We expect such or such a scheme will answer—we are informed that it is disconcerted, and our hopes from it are dashed to pieces: so true is the expression, 'They build too low who build beneath the skies.'

Happiness is not here. There is no rose without a thorn, except the rose of Sharon. Any little happiness we taste in this life is mixed with misery. When we go to the creature for happiness, it disappoints us. The language of our hearts is, 'Oh that I had such a blessing!' When the blessing is granted, we find that it is either very insubstantial or very short-lived. And the more our hearts are knit with affection to any earthly thing, the severer the stroke when we must part—and part we must, for nothing will last always but God.

And the trials of this life, which are common to good and bad, must be borne by all. In some cases, the feelings of the people of God are more exquisite than those of others. If a precious creature is taken from one of them, he is more sensible [conscious] of the loss, because he knew the value of such a jewel. If a wicked person is carried off in his sins, they have more awful apprehensions than others.

If a good man is sick and is deprived of comfort at the same time his distress may be greater than that of a wicked man. We are all born to trouble; and the people of God, so far from being exempted, have their large share of them. When others have ordinary troubles, they have their great tribulations. But they shall come out of them.

4. Persecution on account of religion.

The last tribulation I shall mention is persecution on account of religion.

The apostle Paul assures us, that all that will live godly in Christ Jesus shall suffer persecution. There seems to be a necessary connection between godliness and persecution. There is an enmity between the seed of the woman and the seed of the serpent. In the words of the text, persecution appears to be one of the great tribulations through which they pass. They all suffer persecution in some shape or other. The apostle takes notice of cruel mockings. The greatest philosopher is not proof against bitter taunts and the severe shifts of ridicule. We know human nature. A brave man, who in the day of battle will go up to the mouth of a great gun, feels himself cut to the quick if he hears that a drunkard laughed him to scorn over his bowl, or ridiculed him for some natural defect which he could not help. Ridicule of any kind is severe, but ridicule for religion is still more severe. And if truth cannot find any subject for ridicule in his conduct or in his person, falsehood will never be at a loss to do both.

There is a common species of persecution to which godly clergymen and private Christians are liable, that if people cannot find anything to say against them, they call them weak men. If a private Christian worships God in his family and leads a sober, honest, inoffensive life, he is a weak poor creature, but they believe he is honest and means well, though a perfect bigot. If a clergyman preaches the peculiar doctrines of the gospel, this is enough to fix his character for a weak man. Whereas, if another man should be such a blockhead as that he cannot divide his text into proper heads, he is scarcely taken notice of as a weak man, especially if he can play a hand at cards and take his share of the other bottle. But what is sure to excite the spirit of persecution is to appear against sin. If Christians carry the spirit of religion as far as it will go, they must rebuke sin. If the sinner is rebuked, he becomes an enemy. And when he becomes an enemy he will at last traduce and vilify the Christian for wishing well to his soul.

Let no man suppose that the spirit of persecution is dead. The world is still the enemy of Christ—and the Christian world, as sure and perhaps as much as even the Pagan world was, is against him. It is not the spirit of persecution that is dead, it is only the spirit of Christianity. There are many eulogiums upon the present age for their liberal sentiments, in that none are persecuted for their religious opinions. But it may be asked, 'What will they persecute? Will they persecute people like themselves? Are not religious people just as worldly as foolish, some as social as your carnal people? Will not a religious man in our days drink as many glasses, and talk as much idle discourse upon the Lord's Day, as other people? Do religious people carry the spirit of religion into their dealings? Are they as religious over a glass [of strong drink] as when hearing sermon? Are they as religious when buying or selling as when they are saying their prayers? Does the purity of their lives correspond with the purity of their expressions?' If not, why should people persecute them? Time was when the Church was terrible like an army with banners. People were afraid of religious characters. They lived up to their professions. And if all the religious people did so in our days, they would find to their cost that persecution is not yet dead. The few that are truly religious suffer persecution, but they are so very scarce and so very obscure, that the world do not think it worth their while to take great notice of them. And their hands are weakened when they find that people who have the name of being good men, are so dastardly that they are afraid to rebuke sin. Such a great man would be angry at them, and would not invite them to his table. Another great man promised his interest to his son or nephew—if the Christian rebukes him, he will not do for them.

When this is the spirit of our day, what should bring persecution upon us? The Christian that rebukes sin is a hot-headed enthusiast; the man who shuts his eyes and winks at sin is a worthy, good man—he is none of your narrow bigots who send everybody to perdition but themselves. It is said there is no persecution. We can prove the reverse when the spirit of Christianity shows itself. People are said to be very liberal in their pretensions. But if those liberal-minded people are told the danger of those sins which they live in, will they bear it patiently? They will not! They immediately persecute. If a Christian, by doing his duty, thwarts any of their favourite pursuits, what will be the consequence? That he shall feel their resentment. And if the spirit of Christianity were general in the professors of Christianity, persecution would revive again. A lion or a tiger may be tame enough till he gets something to provoke his rage. But the people of God, at death, are made free from all their troubles and persecutions; they shall enter into rest, and into the joy of their Lord; they shall obtain joy and gladness, and sorrow and sighing shall flee away.

2. How they are prepared for this blessed state

The second thing proposed was to mention the procuring cause of, and the means by which they are prepared for, this blessed state.

They are said to have washed their robes and made them white in the blood of the Lamb. The death of Christ is the procuring cause of their salvation. The chiefest of saints, the very martyrs, are not said to have washed their robes in their own blood. Nothing but the blood of the Saviour can wash away the stain of sin out of the soul, or sanctify the life and conversation. And this appears from the following reasons:

1. The Scripture positively assures us that the blood of bulls and goats could not take away sin, nor could sacrifices and offerings make the people that offered them perfect as to relieving the conscience. Though they should give their first-born for their transgression, and the fruit of their body for the sin of their soul, it would not do. Unconvinced sinners talk a great deal about what God could do, and if he chose himself he might pardon sin without the atonement of Christ. But we might ask them who told them this. We know there are many things which God cannot do: he cannot tell a lie—he cannot do a wrong thing—he cannot offer an insult to one of his own essential attributes—he cannot countenance disorder and confusion. If God was to pardon sin by an absolute act of his absolute almighty power, as these heathens pretend, how would he show his hatred to sin? Though his mercy would be glorified, what would come of his justice, holiness and truth? But in the death and sufferings of Christ, he punishes sin and pardons the sinner in a manner consistent with all his attributes, his perfections are

glorified, and all eternity will ring with the praises of his free illustrious grace.

2. Repentance of itself could not wash our souls or procure our pardon, and this appears from Scripture and experience.

Scripture positively assures us that Judas repented and restored the silver. But as he made no believing application to the blood of Christ, he died in despair, and all his sins about him. We read of several heathens who had terrors of conscience, but nothing could give them comfort as they were strangers to the method and way of salvation. But what is more to the purpose, let the question be asked at all good Christians, and they will acknowledge that repentance alone will not purify the soul, that terror of conscience will only drive to despair, and that nothing will soften them till they apply to the blood of sprinkling.

It is the sufferings of Christ that makes our repentance acceptable to God. Without this, repentance would make us to despair; and repentance is only serviceable when it has recourse to the blood of the Saviour. There may be terror of conscience the first part of repentance, but there cannot be a softening upon the heart till we look to him whom we have pierced with our sins.

3. As this blood is the procuring cause of our happiness, faith is the blessed mean appointed by God for applying the blood to our souls. Faith is the bunch of hyssop that takes this blood and applies it to our consciences, and when we do so, the natural consequence of such an application is peace in the conscience and purity in the mind and obedience in the life. Such a faith purifies the heart, worketh by love, and overcometh the world.

It purifies the affections and setteth them upon the things that are above. It sanctifies the life and conversation and, by a holy course of actions, it prepares the soul for heaven. It is the service of holiness, and holiness qualifies us for happiness. It gives us a relish for the pure, sublime, and spiritual pleasures which are at God's right hand for ever and ever. There is a natural connection between holiness and happiness. Faith does this as it unites us to the Saviour and applies his precious blood to our souls. He that believeth hath the witness in himself. Faith draws fresh supplies out of Christ, and the oftener we apply to him the more holy our souls are—and when we are made perfect in holiness we shall then be admitted to heaven.

3. The blessedness of the saints after death

The third thing proposed was the happy place of the saints after death.

Of this state the Scripture informs us that 'eye hath not seen, ear hath not heard, neither hath it entered into the heart of man to conceive the things which God hath prepared for those who love him.' And though God has condescended to adapt himself to our weak faculties by giving us the most exalted description of the glories of that blessed place, by similes borrowed from the most pleasant and most useful things the lower creation can afford, we can reason about them but darkly. Our reasoning is like the idea which a child, bred in a cottage, would form of a royal palace if it were described to him. But, while we follow Scripture for our guide it refreshes our imagination to meditate upon the glories of those bright mansions which our Redeemer has gone to prepare for us, called in Scripture 'the inheritance of the saints in light'. It is a pleasure to think of the happiness which we shall enjoy in that blessed place, where we shall walk with God high in salvation and the climes of bliss. This pleasure not only refreshes the mind, but likewise purifies the heart, and has a tendency to qualify us for the bright scenes upon which we meditate. A meditation upon heaven will naturally make us wish to enjoy it, and, while we wish to enjoy it, we shall carefully endeavour to prepare ourselves for such a state of joy and happiness.

From the words of the text, we find that the happiness of the saints consists in the following things:

1. They enjoy the presence of God, and serve him for ever and ever,
2. They are made free from all trouble and want.
3. They possess every kind of pleasure and of delight.

1. They enjoy the presence of God, and serve him for ever and ever.

While we dwell in these tabernacles of clay, we see our Creator as it were through a glass darkly, but then we shall see him face to face. We see him through his works and climb, as it were, from the creature to the glorious Creator. We see him still more clearly in his Word when he pleases to enlighten our dark minds. But even this view of him is faint in comparison of that of the saints in light. They see him as he is. This is what we call the beatific vision. Although God Almighty is present everywhere, yet how insensible we are of his presence very often! We go forward, but we do not find him—backward, but we do not see him, so that the language of our experience is, 'O that I knew where to find him!' 'Verily thou art a God that hidest thyself, O God of Israel, the Saviour.' His people often complain of an absent God. This happens when they do not enjoy the comfort of his presence in their souls. Like a cloud intercepting the light of the sun, either guilt upon the conscience or some evil propensity in the will and affections often deprives us of the comfortable presence of God while we are here. But for sin, the mind would be always so clear as that we would see God. And when the mind shall be made free from sin, we shall be as sensible of the comfortable presence of God as we can now be of the presence of anything that strikes our senses. Saints and angels see God in heaven with the eye of the mind, as we see the sun that enlightens this lower creation. They behold him with a rapture of joy, and their faculties are made so strong that they can endure the sight. Our faculties are so weak that we cannot see God and live. The sight would break these clay vessels in pieces. And as we shall enjoy the presence of God, it shall fill our hearts with gladness. 'In thy presence', says the psalmist, 'is fulness of joy, and at thy right hand are pleasures for evermore.' They can call all these pleasures their own. The smallest creature that enjoys the light of the sun can call the light his own. And as they enjoy his presence they serve him in his temple for ever and ever.

If they can say, even in the lower temple, that a day in his courts is better than a thousand, what transport of joy and triumph do they possess in the higher house! They never weary day or night. There is not a material temple there, for God himself is their temple, and the Lord Jesus Christ is the sun that enlightens that happy place. And if a few minutes of the pleasures of religion at solemn occasions make us forget everything, whatever we saw—and if these joys are so ravishing that the time seems short while they continue with us—what are the pleasures which we shall be drinking in for ever and ever?

And as they see him constantly, they cannot but love and admire him. We admire anything that we think has any real or imaginary perfection. In God there is every possible perfection. 'Honour and majesty are before him; strength and beauty are in his sanctuary.' What are honour, majesty, beauty or strength, but emanations from him? And if these dazzle our eyes and attract our admiration, what views do the blessed get of increased beauty, unbounded power, unlimited goodness, unerring wisdom, imperishable grace, and inconceivable glory! The more they see, the more they search, the more they admire, and the more they adore. Upon every new view they get, they fall down before him and ascribe honour, glory and power to him that sitteth upon the throne, and to the Lamb, for ever and ever.

And as his people serve God constantly in heaven, it is probable they may have more solemn and stated times of worship than others. And as knowledge is essential to our intellectual happiness and improvement, it is likely that some of those, who have made greater advances in the knowledge of the works of God and of his attributes, may be appointed to instruct others. And in proper time as they increase in knowledge, they shall increase in happiness.

Their knowledge, and consequently their happiness, will improve gradually. It is not likely that a private Christian, who is admitted to the joys of heaven, should all at once acquire as much knowledge of the works or ways of God as Moses and Elijah, Abraham and Enoch, or any of the saints who have been increasing in knowledge and happiness for some thousands of years. They shall be made acquainted gradually with the wisdom of God which he shows in his Word. All the dark steps of providence shall then be made clear. It shall then be made appear why such-and-such events were permitted to take place. We shall then admire what now appears as a riddle to us. The babe in Christ shall then comprehend what now puzzles the acutest philosopher. We shall understand what are the causes that produced such-and-such effects. The rise and fall of kingdoms and empires, the darkest labyrinth of state intrigues, as well as the most secret histories of individuals who were instrumental in carrying on the most amazing revolutions, shall then be laid open to view. The goodness as well as the justice of God shall be seen in permitting the most atrocious act to be accomplished by the vilest and most wicked of mankind.

If the wisdom of man is seen in a curious piece of mechanism, the manifold wisdom of God shall be seen, not only in the solar system, but through the whole of his works. And as nothing was created in vain, it shall then be understood why such-and-such things were created, and for what useful purposes they were designed. And as the universe is a glorious fabric, the parts of which depend upon one another, we shall be gradually made to understand them. The wonders of creation and providence shall be a never-failing scene of knowledge and admiration to believers. And as this shall form a part of their delightful employment, their gratitude and love shall break forth upon every new discovery, in songs of praise and thanksgiving.

And as creation shall furnish them with songs of praise, we have cause to believe that redemption shall employ their hosannas and hallelujahs for ever and ever. This is a subject the angels have a desire to pry into. And if the works of creation shall always afford some new cause of wonder and delight, we may believe that we shall always make new discoveries of the manifold wisdom and grace of God in the astonishing work of redemption.

And as we upon earth have our daily and weekly stated times of devotion, and besides all this we have our more solemn times to celebrate the dying love of our great Redeemer, who knows but there may be something similar to this in heaven itself? Besides these ordinary times of worship, they may have extraordinary times to celebrate some new discovery in the works and wonders and perfections of God.

And as we may believe there will be no jarring sound in the harmony of heaven, it is probable there will be a universal language spoken there. A question has been agitated among divines, what will be the language of heaven? Some supposed that the Hebrew will be the language spoken—others, that all languages will be spoken in that blessed place. The most rational manner of considering that matter seems to be this. All languages are but certain combinations of sounds to convey certain ideas which are in the mind. Sounds which are very well understood in one place are not understood in another, and consequently cannot convey an idea. But when a person feels any strong sensation, he can make himself understood whatever language he uses.

Disembodied spirits are more free in their motions than spirits confined in bodies, and we may believe they have a short method of communicating their thoughts to one another. The most eloquent orator upon earth will take some considerable time to communicate his thoughts to his audience if he has a matter of great magnitude to lay before them, but we may believe that spirits can instantaneously convey their ideas to each other. And as the use of language is to convey thought, we may believe that all the blessed have this faculty. They understand one another, and agree perfectly in worshipping God with all their heart and soul.

And we may likewise conclude, both from Scripture and reason, that as they shall know one another and agree perfectly without ceasing in the worship and service of God, that they shall be differently employed. Some have a pleasure in one kind of speculation, some in another. There are moral, natural and mathematical truths, and there are peculiar pleasures arising from the investigation of each. And though all the blessed are completely holy to the utmost extent of their faculties, what should hinder us to believe that there are particular virtues and graces which they particularly take delight in? They do not spend an idle eternity; they employ their faculties in his praise and they will be rewarded according to their works. One star is different from another in glory—they all shine, but we see some larger than others. It is thus in heaven. There are some there that shine like stars of the first magnitude—they have been eminent for grace and godliness, and are therefore advanced to the highest dignities in the kingdom of God. They are next the throne. Others shine with a less degree of lustre, but they are all happy as heart can wish. They all pursue the same great interest, and all worship and serve the same great God, but not all in the same degree.

There is a variety of enjoyments and of employments among the blessed. Some cultivate one faculty and some another. And though they form one great society, and are completely happy in enjoying the company of each other, still we may believe that there will be separate parties of pleasure among them. A schoolboy, though he were the son of a prince, is not a fit companion for a philosopher, and yet both may be equally happy in prosecuting their respective studies. In like manner the good Christian, who has been admitted yesterday or the day before to the joys of paradise, is not a fit companion for Abraham—he has not such a measure of knowledge or of grace as to fit him for such a high degree of glory. But he shall meet with thousands of his own rank, and with these he shall delight to associate. We must believe that there is the utmost regularity in the economy of the higher house: there are several mansions prepared according to their several capacities—every place is properly adjusted—every star shines in its own proper orb.

And though all the heavenly host are completely happy in thus worshipping God in his temple, and associating together, what makes up the sum total of their bliss is that they see the face of God without a veil. The greater vessels draw in greater draughts of pleasure, but every vessel is full. Some are nearer to the Sun of righteousness, but all see him as he is. And what seals their happiness is that it is to last for ever. They worship him for ever in his temple. And may not we adopt the language of the Queen of Sheba, 'How happy are they thy servants!' Such as get there may say it was a true report they heard upon earth, but the one half was not told them. But what constitutes the chief part of their happiness is the enjoyment of God himself. Beyond this we cannot form a wish. May God grant that we may know from experience what it means!

2. They are made free from all trouble and want.

Again, another part of their happiness is, that they shall be free from all trouble and want. One of the great evils attending straitened circumstances is hunger and thirst. Poverty shall not be known in these happy continents. And not only are hunger and thirst painful sensations in themselves, but the very fear of them will make us unhappy. In these blissful regions they shall enjoy peace and plenty. They shall feed upon angels' food. What that is we do not know, unless it be the Word of God: 'Man liveth not by bread alone, but by every word that proceedeth out of the mouth of God.' We know by experience that a piece of bread is a natural means to support our life. Bread is a dead thing in itself, and it could not do this but for the divine appointment. In heaven we shall eat the bread of life, and for this we ought to labour.

But I must observe that every enjoyment there is to be understood in a spiritual sense. Thus, when we are told of eating and drinking in the kingdom of God, we are not to understand that it is in a carnal way. If a feast would afford a gratification to an appetite, when we get to heaven we may indulge our spiritual appetites to the full. There is no danger of excess there. Their desires are not attended with uneasiness, because they have immediate fruition. Have they a desire for drink? They have rivers of pleasure. Have they a desire for food? They have the heavenly manna, the milk and the honey of Canaan, and access to the tree of life, which is in the midst of the garden of God, and of which they may eat and live for ever. Hunger and thirst with us are uneasy feelings. In that place they have no experience of what they mean.

They have not the smallest trouble. The heat or the light does not annoy them. In this life the greatest blessing we enjoy, if we have too much of it, is a source of uneasiness. Though summer is a most pleasant time of the year, we know that a very warm day is disagreeable—the heat will annoy us. And though it is a pleasant thing to behold the sun, we sometimes complain of having too much of it. Excess of heat is disagreeable, as is excess of cold.

In that blessed country, the seasons are always of the most agreeable temperature. They have no storms or tempests, no disagreeable heat or cold—nothing to molest them. They have constant temperate seasons and a serene sky. They are not afraid of old age or wrinkles, for the tree of life keeps them always young. They are strangers to sickness and death, and the voice of sorrow is never heard in their streets. They always enjoy health, beauty and vigour. There is pleasure in every face, and joy in every countenance. There is no murmur or discontent, any cause of complaint, or any grievance to redress. Their former sorrows are turned to joy, and their tears of distress to songs of triumph. Their harps, which in the days of their captivity they often hung upon the willow-trees, are now tuned to sing the song of Moses and of the Lamb. All their miseries are at an end for God himself, with his own gentle hand, shall wipe away all tears from their eyes. Their heavy hearts are made light from the burden of sin, and like a man whom his mother comforteth, the great Father of mercies shall speak comfort to the children of Zion.

The rod of oppression and the lash of tyranny do not gall them any more. The poor man is not any longer in danger of being turned out of his precarious dwelling, nor is the debtor in danger of being shut up in prison by the cruel and unrelenting hand of his creditors. Friends that meet in the happy circle will not feel the severe pangs of separation, and the dear departed relation, for whom we have mourned and wept, shall meet us there to part no more for ever.

Our poor, virtuous and religious friends, whom we sometimes helped with our means, and who in return helped us with their prayers, shall receive us into their everlasting habitations. The persons for whom we shed silent tears, and over whom our hearts melted with tenderness and sympathy, shall forget all their sorrows when they taste but one drop of the new wine in their Father's kingdom.

The perverse rebel for whom we wrestled in prayer at a throne of grace, shall perhaps be among the first to welcome us when we land upon Emmanuel's shore, and shall shame us out of our unbelief by asking do we now believe that the Lord is a prayer-hearing God? The prodigal son and the ungodly relation for whom we have cried in agony to God to save their souls from perdition, it is likely, may astonish us when we look up above us, and hear them singing with a loud voice, 'Unto him that loved us, and washed us from our sins in his own blood, and hath made us kings and priests unto God and his Father, to him be glory and dominion for ever and ever. Amen.'

3. They shall possess every kind of pleasure and of delight.

But in the last place, they shall possess every kind of pleasure and of delight. It is expressly said, that he that sitteth upon the throne shall dwell among them. It is likewise said in another place that God hath prepared a city for them. The great men of the earth, who seem to themselves to have monopolized all the happiness in it to their own use, seem to think that this same happiness consists in living alternately in the city and in the country. The people of God have a heavenly city and a heavenly country. The city is said to be 1500 miles long and 1500 miles broad, an extent of ground containing a greater number of square miles than the whole Roman Empire. The very streets of it are said to be paved with gold, and the foundation to be garnished with all manner of precious stones, and the twelve gates are said to be twelve pearls. When the Holy Ghost makes use of such magnificent images, it is to raise our thoughts to that blessed place. Imagination here has full scope. The city is likewise a paradise. A river of the water of life passed through the midst of it, and on each side of it is the tree of life.

Nothing refreshes the imagination more than smiling meadows, purling streams, murmuring brooks and pleasant cascades, and therefore the Saviour is said to lead his people unto living fountains of water.

And as where is a city there is a country. If the city is glorious beyond conception, though imagination should go to the utmost stretch, we cannot form an idea of the beauty of the country. What are the glories of Lebanon, Sharon and Carmel, the delightful landscapes of Arabia Felix, or even the garden of God in Eden, though we saw it compared to the heavenly country? He leads them unto living fountains of water. He shows them all the beautiful prospects of the heavenly Canaan. He bids them look as far as sight can reach or thought can stretch, and he tells them the whole is his own. The Lord is their shepherd, they shall not want; he maketh them lie down in green pastures, and leadeth them beside the still waters. They have fountains of life, trees of life and rivers of pleasure. They have the river of life, and on each side of it the tree of life yielding fruit every month.

They cannot possibly be sick, for the leaves of the tree of life are for the healing of the nations.

They have formerly, when in their house of pilgrimage, made use of the fruit for food to their souls, and applied the leaves to the wounds which are made in their consciences. Their cure was completed at death, and now the fruit keeps them always young and healthful, wholesome and cheerful. And that nothing may be wanting [lacking] to complete their happiness, the Lamb who is in the midst of the throne feedeth them. They enjoy a continual feast and form a blessed and a happy society, for they perfectly agree in sentiment. They are perfectly holy, and therefore humble. There is no strife for rank and precedence, for the Saviour himself has adjusted the ceremonial. Everyone knows the rank to which he is entitled, and his own seat at his Father's table. He does not envy those above him, or despise those below him. They all see the King in his beauty at the head of the table. They enjoy his conversation and are happy in his smile. There is neither envy nor pride in heavenly minds. The highest will condescend to speak to the lowest. The soul who moves in a lower sphere will not envy him who moves in a higher, or wish that he had been placed where he is. The saint of the lower order knows that he could not properly act but where he is. A saint of small degree knows that he could not praise God for doing for him such great things as he has done for Abraham, Moses or Elijah, nor can he thank God that he has given him as great a measure of grace and happiness. But they all agree in the joyful sound of salvation, and thus far they are all upon an equal footing. They all obtain as much happiness as they can wish or receive.

They feed upon angels' food, they feast upon the favour of God, and are satisfied with those delicious banquets which are the proper food of spirits. The table shall never be withdrawn; it is always full. The feast is always beginning. They have music at the feast, and all join in the harmony. They are happy in the conversation of each other. There is not an idle or foolish word spoken there. They do not talk upon useless or trivial subjects. Their conversation is edifying, such as is fit for God to hear and approve. They talk of the great acts of God and the wonderful deeds of his right hand. They talk of their own happy experience, and what he has done for them. The one will, it is probable, entertain the other with the history of his own conversion, and what God has done for himself and others. Creation, providence and redemption will always afford subjects of conversation. At this feast the glories of the Godhead will shine upon them with full lustre, and they shall be transformed into his image. They shall drink at the fountainhead of joy and be satisfied with his likeness. And thus their happiness is to continue and increase through the endless ages of eternity. And may the God of all grace prepare us for relishing all these heavenly joys!

4. Application

I conclude with some practical improvement.

1. The way to these glorious mansions, of which I have been endeavouring to give a faint description, is through the gate of death. It is like a passage underground to some beautiful palace. You have heard the cause of my choosing this subject—I mean the death of my sister. Praise from such a near relation would be no panegyric. It gives me pleasure, however, that others will do

this for me. She had the fear of God from her youth, and this thought is a gleam of joy across my breast and prevents my indulging any melancholy on account of her death. Instead of shedding tears for her, I should shed tears for myself. I am in a body of sin and death. 'The Lord gave, and the Lord hath taken away; blessed be the name of the Lord.' He has a right to his jewels any time he chooses to call for them. The language of providence to you, my friends, when you hear of the death of any valuable and worthy person, is to be followers of those who through faith and patience are now inheriting the promises. If you live such a life, you shall die such a death. Go you, and do likewise.

2. I have been describing to you the joys of heaven. And as you all hope to go to that blessed place, that you may not be disappointed in your hope, permit me to give you a good advice.

The obedience of Christ is what procured heaven for his people. Remember, therefore, that he is the author of eternal salvation to those who obey him. If he obeyed for you, it is your duty to obey him. The obedience he requires is that you believe you have great need of a Saviour, and cannot do without one. When you believe you are lost sinners, the next duty he requires of you is to trust in himself entirely for your salvation. When you trust then in the Saviour, you shall taste of his love. And the next and last duty he requires of you is that you fulfil the law from this principle of love—that you love God and man—that you perform duty and avoid sin in his own strength. And if you thus depend upon him he promises to lead you safe to glory.

But some poor soul will say, 'Alas! I cannot believe thus in my Saviour.' Very true! Attempt it, however, and look up to himself for strength. They that wait upon the Lord shall renew their strength, and go on from strength to strength till they arrive at last safe in Zion. Holiness is the high road to heaven.

3. Lastly, You have heard there are different mansions in heaven. This is no encouragement to the lazy Christian who says he would be content with any place there. Such as say this, it is to be feared, prepare for no place in it. If any person thinks he has made progress enough already, and that he is good enough for heaven and will get there as soon as others who make more noise about it, this is a sad proof that he has not yet set his face toward Zion. Such as go to heaven have some concern about it. If you are without concern, pray to God to awaken you.

Again, this is no discouragement to the weak Christian who fears that he cannot be a companion for Abraham. If you were admitted to the king's table, would you complain that lords and dukes sat above you? There are degrees in glory. The highest there speak to the lowest, and the Saviour speaks to them all— and it is a part of their happiness that one is higher than another. They all make progress in perfection and holiness; the lower orders imitate the higher and follow their example, and the higher and lower imitate God. Holiness is the great aim of the Church, militant and triumphant. Let us cultivate holiness, that we may say at last, 'O death, where is thy sting? O grave, where is thy victory?' Let us cultivate holiness that we may be qualified to sing the song of triumph: 'To him that loved us, and washed us in his blood, and made us kings and priests to God, be honour and glory for ever and ever. Amen!'

May God bless his Word.

Heaven

Lines occasioned by the death of his sister

Great King of saints and angels bright,
Who once didst dwell in clay,
Our battles thou didst bravely fight,
And thou hast gained the day.

For us a place thou didst prepare,
A city great and high,
Bright palaces, and mansions fair
Beyond the sun and sky.

No man nor angel can describe
The joys that there abound;
Friendship is there, and happiness
In full perfection found.

Let thought and fancy take their flight
As far as each can go,
And these describe a happiness
Such as they find below.

Description fails, and boldest thought
Falls short of what is there.
Who can describe infinitude?
Thy glories who declare?

Bliss, glory, light and happiness,
And purest love divine
Are found within thy palaces,
And in thy courts do shine.

Rivers of pleasures and of joy,
And living fountains flow:
On ev'ry side the tree of life
For food and health does grow.

The angels, eldest sons of light.
Loud hallelujahs sing,
And all the elect multitude
Exalt their Lord and King.

Salvation, that delightful theme,
Does all their harps employ;
This fills their souls with ecstasy;
This fills their hearts with joy.

My dearest Mary, you are now
Among the chosen race;
You join your voice with those that cry,
'Salvation is of grace!'

O voice of triumph and of joy!
When shall I hear the sound?
When shall I see Jerusalem?
When shall my joys abound?

O blessed Jesus, show thy face,
And give me grace and love;
And give me new obedience,

And fix my thoughts above.

O blessed Salem, glorious place,
Where all the elect meet,
And saints and seraphs throw their crowns,
Sweet Jesus, at thy feet!

This is the city of our God,
The paradise of joy;
And to prepare us for the place.
May we our life employ!

O Jesus, wash us in thy blood;
From sin our souls set free;
And send thy angels at our death
To bring our souls to thee!

What tongue can speak, what thought can reach
The joys thou hast in store!
And if I saw thy beauteous face,
My soul would ask no more.

L - #0159 - 150721 - C0 - 210/148/7 - PB - DID3128895